TWELVE EXTRAORDINARY WOMEN

HOW GOD SHAPED WOMEN *of the* BIBLE, *and* WHAT HE WANTS *to* DO *with* YOU

JOHN MACARTHUR

THOMAS NELSON
Since 1798

NASHVILLE   DALLAS   MEXICO CITY   RIO DE JANEIRO   BEIJING

Published in Nashville, Tennessee, by Thomas Nelson.
Thomas Nelson is a registered trademark of Thomas Nelson, Inc.

Published in association with the literary agency of Wolgemuth & Associates, Inc.

Thomas Nelson, Inc. titles may be purchased in bulk for educational, business, fund-raising, or sales promotional use. For information, please e-mail SpecialMarkets@ThomasNelson.com.

Scripture quotations noted NASB are taken from THE NEW AMERICAN STANDARD BIBLE®, © The Lockman Foundation 1960, 1962, 1963, 1968, 1971, 1972, 1973, 1975, 1977. Used by permission. (www.Lockman.org)

Scripture quotations marked NKJV are taken from the NEW KING JAMES VERSION®. © 1982 by Thomas Nelson, Inc. Used by permission. All rights reserved.

Quotations marked KJV are from the King James Version of the Bible.

Library of Congress Cataloging-in-Publication Data

MacArthur, John, 1939–
Twelve extraordinary women : how God shaped women of the Bible and what He wants to do with you / John MacArthur.
p. cm.
ISBN 978-0-7852-6256-5 (HC)
ISBN 978-0-7852-8354-6 (IE)
ISBN 978-1-4002-8028-5 (TP)
1. Women in the Bible—Biography. 2. Women in the Bible—Meditations.
3. Christian women—Religious life. I. Title.
BS575.M26 2005
220.9'2'082—dc22
2005021006

Printed in the United States of America

09 10 11 12 13 RRD 12 11 10 9 8

DEDICATION

To all the little girls in my life, my granddaughters, who are on the way to becoming, by God's grace, extraordinary women:

Kathryn

Olivia

Kylee

Jessica

Susannah

Gracie

Brooke

Elizabeth

Audrey

ACKNOWLEDGMENTS

I am grateful for and indebted to Phil Johnson, who has again, as so often before, applied his remarkable editorial skills to my material. For this book, he has done far more than that, by adding his own rich insights to those chapters where my meager material was inadequate.

And very special thanks goes to my extraordinary Patricia, who has faithfully supported this ordinary man through forty-two years of marriage.

CONTENTS

PREFACE

I never anticipated that my book on the apostles *(Twelve Ordinary Men)* would be as well received by readers as it was. People seemed to appreciate and enjoy the character-study format, even though it is a slight departure from my normal expository style. The book's method and arrangement seemed particularly well suited to small-group studies, and that might have helped fuel a still wider interest. Perhaps even more significant was the intensely practical and personal relevance of such character studies. It helps, I think, to see the apostles as they were: *ordinary* men. That was, after all, the whole point of the book. These were men anyone can relate to. Most of us can easily see aspects of our own character in their personalities, their shortcomings, their struggles, their frequent blunders, and their longing to be everything Christ wanted them to be. It gives us great hope to see how wonderfully God used people such as these.

After *Twelve Ordinary Men* had been on the bestseller lists for more than a year, my friends at Thomas Nelson suggested a sequel. Why not deal in a similar format with the lives of twelve of the principal women of Scripture? Everyone who heard the idea was immediately enthusiastic about it. Thus the volume you hold in your hands was born.

Of course, there were no decisions to be made about whom to feature in the first book. *Jesus* chose His twelve disciples; all I had to do was research their lives and write about them. This new book would be a different matter. Faced with a plethora of extraordinary women in the Bible, I made a long list of possibilities. The task of narrowing the roll to twelve was by no means easy. I weighed their relative importance in biblical history and chose twelve women who were critical to the story of redemption.

I hope you'll agree that my final short-list includes a good variety of personality types and an interesting assortment of truly extraordinary women. My hope is that, as with the first book, readers will see aspects of themselves in these studies and be encouraged by the reminder that our personal struggles and temptations are the very same kinds of trials that all believers in all ages have confronted. Thus we are reminded that even in the midst of our trouble, God remains eternally faithful (1 Cor. 10:13). The God of Abraham, Isaac, and Jacob is the God of Sarah, Rebekah, and Rachel too. He is also the God of every believer in *our* generation—men and women alike. We, like all of them, have our shortcomings. But we are His people and the sheep of His pasture (Ps. 100:3). And His faithfulness *still* reaches to the clouds (Ps. 36:5).

Some have already asked me the significance of the delicate shift in titles. If the disciples were "ordinary," how is it that these twelve women are *extra*ordinary?

The answer, of course, is that while the disciples were ordinary in one sense, they were also *extraordinary* in another sense. As far as their innate talents and their human backgrounds are concerned, they were genuinely ordinary, and deliberately so. "God has chosen the foolish things of the world to put to shame the wise, and God has chosen the weak things of the world to put to shame the things which are mighty; and the base things of the world and the things which are despised God has chosen, and the things which are not, to bring to nothing the things that are, that no flesh should glory in His presence" (1 Cor. 1:27–29 NKJV). It was only Christ's work in the disciples' lives that gave them such remarkable power and influence, so that what they became was something quite uncommon—and what they accomplished (Acts 17:6) was something truly extraordinary.

The same thing is true with the women featured in this book. Most of them were unremarkable in and of themselves. They were ordinary, common, and in some cases shockingly low-caste women—in exactly the same way the disciples were common men. Take the Samaritan woman of John 4, for instance. We don't even know her name. Likewise, Anna was an obscure, elderly widow who appears in only one brief vignette in the opening of Luke (2:36–38). Rahab was a common harlot. Even Mary, the mother of Christ, was a young girl of no particular distinction, living in an obscure town in a barren and despised district of Galilee. In each instance, what made them extraordinary was a memorable, life-changing encounter with the God of the universe.

The only real exception is Eve, who *began* life as someone quite extraordinary in every way. She was created by God to be the pure and pristine ideal of womanhood. But she soon spoiled it by sinning. Still, she, too, became a living depiction of the truth that God can recover and redeem those who fall—and make them truly extraordinary trophies of His grace in spite of their failures. In fact, I'm convinced that by God's redeeming grace, the person Eve will be through all eternity is far *more* glorious than she was in her original earthly innocence.

In other words, all these women ultimately became extraordinary not because of any natural qualities of their own, but because the one true God whom they worshiped is great, mighty, glorious, and awesome, and *He* refined them like silver. He redeemed them through the work of an extraordinary Savior—His own divine Son—and conformed them to His image (Rom. 8:29). In other words, the gracious work of God in their lives made each one of these women truly extraordinary.

They therefore stand as reminders of both our fallenness and our potential. Speaking together as one, they all point us to Christ. In every case, He was the One to whom they looked for salvation. We'll see, for example, how Eve, Sarah, Rahab, and Ruth were all in the line of descent that would produce the Promised One who would crush the serpent's head. Hannah likewise longed for a Savior and rejoiced in the promise of salvation. In fact, Hannah's words of praise about the Savior (1 Sam. 2:1–10) are echoed in Mary's Magnificat. That, of course, was Mary's outpouring of praise when she first learned that she would finally be the one—blessed by God above all other women—to give birth to the Savior. Anna, who had hoped for the Savior all her life, was blessed in her old age to be one of the very first to recognize Him in His infancy (Luke 2:36–38). All the other women featured in this book became some of His earliest disciples. Every one of them therefore testifies to us about Christ.

My prayer for you is that as you read this book you will share their faith, imitate their faithfulness, and learn to love the Savior whose work in their lives made them truly extraordinary. Your life can be extraordinary, too, by His wonderful grace.

INTRODUCTION

Oone of the unique features of the Bible is the way it exalts women. Far from ever demeaning or belittling women, Scripture often seems to go out of the way to pay homage to them, to ennoble their roles in society and family, to acknowledge the importance of their influence, and to exalt the virtues of women who were particularly godly examples.

From the very first chapter of the Bible, we are taught that women, like men, bear the stamp of God's own image (Gen. 1:27; 5:1–2). Women play prominent roles in many key biblical narratives. Wives are seen as venerated partners and cherished companions to their husbands, not merely slaves or pieces of household furniture (Gen. 2:20–24; Prov. 19:14; Eccl. 9:9). At Sinai, God commanded children to honor *both* father and mother (Ex. 20:12). That was a revolutionary concept in an era when most pagan cultures were dominated by men who ruled their households with an iron fist while women were usually regarded as lesser creatures—mere servants to men.

Of course, the Bible recognizes divinely ordained role distinctions between men and women—many of which are perfectly evident from the circumstances of creation alone. For example, women have a unique and vital role in childbearing and nurturing little ones. Women themselves also have a particular need for support and protection, because physically, they are "weaker vessels" (1 Peter 3:7 NKJV). Scripture establishes the proper order in the family and in the church accordingly, assigning the duties of headship and protection in the home to husbands (Eph. 5:23) and appointing men in the church to the teaching and leadership roles (1 Tim. 2:11–15).

Yet women are by no means marginalized or relegated to any second-class status (Gal. 3:28). On the contrary, Scripture seems to set women apart for special honor (1 Peter 3:7). Husbands are commanded to love their wives sacrificially, as Christ loves the church—even, if necessary, at the cost of their own lives (Eph. 5:25–31). The Bible acknowledges and celebrates the priceless value of a virtuous woman (Prov. 12:4; 31:10; 1 Cor. 11:7). In other words, from cover to cover, the Bible portrays women as *extraordinary.*

The biblical accounts of the patriarchs always give due distinction to their wives. Sarah, Rebekah, and Rachel all loom large in the Genesis account of God's dealings with their husbands. Miriam, sister of Moses and Aaron, was both a prophetess and a songwriter—and in Micah 6:4, God Himself honors her alongside her brothers as one of the nation's leaders during the Exodus. Deborah, also a prophetess, was a judge in Israel prior to the monarchy (Judg. 4:4). Scriptural accounts of family life often put wives in the position of wise counselors to their husbands (Judg. 13:23; 2 Kings 4:8–10). When Solomon became king, he publicly paid homage to his mother, standing when she entered his presence, then bowing to her before he sat on his throne (1 Kings 2:19). Sarah and Rahab are expressly named among the heroes of faith in Hebrews 11. Moses' mother (Jochebed) is included as well by implication (v. 23). In Proverbs, wisdom is personified as a woman. The New Testament church is likewise represented as a woman, the bride of Christ.

In the social and religious life of Israel and the New Testament church, women were never relegated to the background. They partook with men in all the feasts and public worship of Israel (Deut. 16:14; Neh. 8:2–3). Women were not required to be veiled or silent in the public square, as they are in some Middle Eastern cultures even today (Gen. 12:14; 24:16; 1 Sam. 1:12). Mothers (not merely fathers) shared teaching responsibilities and authority over their children (Prov. 1:8; 6:20). Women could even be landowners in Israel (Num. 27:8; Prov. 31:16). In fact, wives were expected to administer many of the affairs of their own households (Prov. 14:1; 1 Tim. 5:9–10, 14).

All of that stands in sharp contrast to the way other ancient cultures routinely degraded and debased women. Women in pagan societies during biblical times were often treated with little more dignity than animals. Some of the best-known Greek philosophers—considered the brightest minds of their era—taught that women are inferior creatures by nature. Even in the Roman Empire (perhaps the very pinnacle of pre-Christian civilization) women were usually regarded as mere chattel—personal possessions of their husbands or fathers, with hardly any better standing than household slaves. That, once again, was vastly different from the Hebrew (and biblical) concepts of marriage as a joint inheritance, and parenthood as a partnership where *both* father and mother are to be revered and obeyed by the children (Lev. 19:3).

Pagan *religion* tended to fuel and encourage the devaluation of women even more. Of course, Greek and Roman mythology had its goddesses (such as Diana and Aphrodite). But don't imagine for a moment that goddess-worship in any way raised the status of women in society. The opposite was true. Most temples devoted to goddesses were served by sacred prostitutes—priestesses who sold themselves for money, supposing they were performing a religious sacrament. Both the mythology and the practice of pagan religion has usually been overtly demeaning to women. Male pagan deities were capricious and sometimes wantonly misogynistic. Religious ceremonies were often blatantly obscene—including such things as erotic fertility rites, drunken temple orgies, perverted homosexual practices, and, in the very worst cases, even human sacrifices.

Christianity, born in a world where Roman and Hebrew cultures intersected, elevated the status of women to an unprecedented height. Jesus' disciples included several women (Luke 8:1–3), a practice almost unheard of among the rabbis of His day. Not only that, He *encouraged* their discipleship by portraying it as something more needful than domestic service (Luke 10:38–42). In fact, Christ's first recorded explicit disclosure of His own identity as the true Messiah was made to a Samaritan woman (John 4:25–26). He always treated women with the utmost dignity—even women who might otherwise be regarded as outcasts (Matt. 9:20–22; Luke 7:37–50; John 4:7–27). He blessed their children (Luke 18:15–16), raised their dead (Luke 7:12–15), forgave their sins (Luke 7:44–48), and restored their virtue and honor (John 8:4–11). Thus he exalted the position of womanhood itself.

It is no surprise, therefore, that women became prominent in the ministry of the early church (Acts 12:12–15; 1 Cor. 11:11–15). On the day of Pentecost, when the New Testament church was born, women were there with the chief disciples, praying (Acts 1:12–14). Some were renowned for their good deeds (Acts 9:36); others for their hospitality (Acts 12:12; 16:14–15); still others for their understanding of sound doctrine and their spiritual giftedness (Acts 18:26; 21:8–9). John's second epistle was addressed to a prominent woman in one of the churches under his oversight. Even the apostle Paul, sometimes falsely caricatured by critics of Scripture as a male chauvinist, regularly ministered alongside women (Phil. 4:3). He recognized and applauded their faithfulness and their giftedness (Rom. 16:1–6; 2 Tim. 1:5).

Naturally, as Christianity began to influence Western society, the status of women was dramatically improved. One of the early church fathers, Tertullian, wrote a work titled *On the Apparel of Women* sometime near the end of the second century. He said pagan women who wore elaborate hair ornaments, immodest clothing, and body decorations had actually been forced by society and fashion to abandon the superior splendor of true femininity. He noted, by way of contrast, that as the church had grown and the gospel had borne fruit, one of the visible results was the rise of a trend toward modesty in women's dress and a corresponding elevation of the status of women. He acknowledged that pagan men commonly complained, "Ever since she became a Christian, she walks in poorer garb!"[1] Christian women even became known as "modesty's priestesses."[2] But, Tertullian said, as believers who lived under the lordship of Christ, women were spiritually wealthier, more pure, and thus more glorious than the most extravagant women in pagan society. Clothed "with the silk of uprightness, the fine linen of holiness, the purple of modesty,"[3] they elevated feminine virtue to an unprecedented height.

Even the pagans recognized that. Chrysostom, perhaps the most eloquent preacher of the fourth century, recorded that one of his teachers, a pagan philosopher named Libanius, once said: "Heavens! what women you Christians have!"[4] What prompted Libanius's outburst was hearing how Chrysostom's mother had remained chaste for more than two decades since becoming a widow at age twenty. As the influence of Christianity was felt more and more, women were less and less vilified or mistreated as objects for the amusement of men. Instead, women began to be honored for their virtue and faith.

In fact, Christian women converted out of pagan society were automatically freed from a host of demeaning practices. Emancipated from the public debauchery of temples and theaters (where women were systematically dishonored and devalued), they rose to prominence in home and church, where they were honored and admired for feminine virtues like hospitality, ministry to the sick, the care and nurture of their own families, and the loving labor of their hands (Acts 9:39).

After the Roman emperor Constantine was converted in 312 AD, Christianity was granted legal status in Rome and soon became the dominant religion throughout the Empire. One of the measurable early results of this change was a whole new legal status for women. Rome passed laws recognizing the property rights of women. Legislation governing marriage was revised, so that marriage was legally seen as a partnership, rather than a virtual state of servitude for the wife. In the pre-Christian era, Roman men had power to divorce their wives for virtually any cause, or even for no cause at all. New laws made divorce more difficult, while giving women legal rights against husbands who were guilty of infidelity. Philandering husbands, once an accepted part of Roman society, could no longer sin against their wives with impunity.

This has always been the trend. Wherever the gospel has spread, the social, legal, and spiritual status of women has, as a rule, been elevated. When the gospel has been eclipsed (whether by repression, false religion, secularism, humanistic philosophy, or spiritual decay within the church), the status of women has declined accordingly.

Even when secular movements have arisen claiming to be concerned with women's rights, their efforts have generally been detrimental to the status of women. The feminist movement of our generation, for example, is a case in point. Feminism has devalued and defamed *femininity*. Natural gender distinctions are usually downplayed, dismissed, despised, or denied. As a result, women are now being sent into combat situations, subjected to grueling physical labor once reserved for men, exposed to all kinds of indignities in the workplace, and otherwise encouraged to act and talk like men. Meanwhile, modern feminists heap scorn on women who want family and household to be their first priorities—disparaging the role of motherhood, the one calling that is most uniquely and exclusively feminine. The whole message of feminist egalitarianism is that there is really nothing extraordinary about women.

That is certainly not the message of Scripture. As we have seen, Scripture honors women *as women,* and it encourages them to seek honor in a uniquely feminine way (Prov. 31:10–30).

Scripture never discounts the female intellect, downplays the talents and abilities of women, or discourages the right use of women's spiritual gifts. But whenever the Bible expressly talks about the marks of an excellent woman, the stress is always on feminine *virtue.* The most significant women in Scripture were influential not because of their careers, but because of their *character.* The message these women collectively give is not about "gender equality"; it's about true feminine excellence. And this is always exemplified in moral and spiritual qualities rather than by social standing, wealth, or physical appearance.

According to the apostle Peter, for instance, true feminine beauty is not about external adornment, "arranging the hair, wearing gold, or putting on fine apparel"; *real* beauty is seen instead in "the hidden person of the heart . . . the incorruptible beauty of a gentle and quiet spirit, which is very precious in the sight of God" (1 Peter 3:3–4 NKJV). Paul, likewise, said godliness and good works are the real essence of feminine beauty; not artificial embellishments applied to the outside (1 Tim. 2:9–10). That truth is exemplified to one degree or another by every woman featured in this book.

The *faithfulness* of these women is their true, lasting legacy. I hope as you meet them in Scripture and get to know more about their lives and characters, they will challenge you, motivate you, encourage you, and inspire you with love for the God whom they trusted and served. May your heart be set ablaze with the very same faith, may your life be characterized by a similar faithfulness, and may your soul be overwhelmed with love for the extraordinary God they worshiped.

1

EVE: MOTHER OF ALL LIVING

Adam called his wife's name Eve, because she was the mother of all living.

—Genesis 3:20 NKJV

E ve must have been a creature of unsurpassed beauty. She was the crown and the pinnacle of God's amazing creative work. The first female of Adam's race was the last living thing to be called into existence—actually fashioned directly by the Creator's own hand in a way that showed particular care and attention to detail. Remember, Eve wasn't made out of dust like Adam, but carefully designed from living flesh and bone. Adam was refined dirt; Eve was a glorious refinement of humanity itself. She was a special gift to Adam. She was the necessary partner who finally made his existence complete—and whose own existence finally signaled the completion of all creation.

Eve, the *only* being ever directly created by God from the living tissue of another creature, was indeed a singular marvel. God had composed a vast universe of wonders out of nothing. Then He made Adam from a handful of dust. But nothing in the whole expanse of the universe was more wonderful than this woman made from a handful of Adam. If the man represented the supreme species (a race of creatures made in the image of God), Eve was the living embodiment of humanity's glory (1 Cor. 11:7). God had truly saved the best for last. Nothing else would have sufficed quite so perfectly to be the finishing touch and the very zenith of all creation.

In her original state, undefiled by any evil, unblemished by any disease or defect, unspoiled by any imperfection at all, Eve was the flawless archetype of feminine excellence. She was magnificent in every way. Since no other woman has ever come unfallen into a curse-free world, no other woman could possibly surpass Eve's grace, charm, virtue, ingenuity, intelligence, wit, and pure innocence. Physically, too, she must have personified all the best traits of both strength and beauty. There is no doubt that she was a living picture of sheer radiance.

Scripture, however, gives us no physical description of Eve. Her beauty—splendid as it *must* have been—is never mentioned or even alluded to. The focus of the biblical account is on Eve's duty to her Creator and her role alongside her husband. That is a significant fact, reminding us that the chief distinguishing traits of true feminine excellence are nothing superficial. Women who are obsessed with image, cosmetics, body shapes, and other external matters have a distorted view of femininity. Indeed, Western culture as a whole (including a large segment of the visible church) seems hopelessly confused about these very issues. We need to go back to Scripture to see what God's ideal for a woman really is. And the biblical account of Eve is an excellent reminder of what a woman's true priorities ought to be.

As "the mother of all living," Eve is obviously a major character in the story of humanity's fall and redemption. Yet in all of Scripture, her *name* is used only four times—twice in the Old Testament (Gen. 3:20; 4:1), and twice in the New Testament (2 Cor. 11:3; 1 Tim. 2:13). Not only is no physical description of her given; we don't even know such details as how many children she had, how long she lived, or where and how she died (Gen. 5:3–5). The way Scripture tells her story, almost in abbreviated fashion, helps us focus more clearly on the aspects of her life that have the most significance.

Although Scripture is silent about many things we might like to know about Eve, we are given detailed accounts of her creation, her temptation and fall, the curse that was placed on her, and the subsequent hope that she clung to. Naturally, that's where we'll focus our study of this truly extraordinary woman.

HER CREATION

The biblical account of Eve's remarkable creation is given in Genesis 2:20–25:

> *So Adam gave names to all cattle, to the birds of the air, and to every beast of the field. But for Adam there was not found a helper comparable to him. And the LORD God caused a deep sleep to fall on Adam, and he slept; and He took one of his ribs, and closed up the flesh in its place. Then the rib which the LORD God had taken from man He made into a woman, and He brought her to the man. And Adam said: "This is now bone of my bones and flesh of my flesh; she shall be called Woman, because she was taken out of Man." Therefore a man shall leave his father and mother and be joined to his wife, and they shall become one flesh. And they were both naked, the man and his wife, and were not ashamed.* (NKJV)

In other words, God performed a surgical procedure on Adam. Scripture describes the operation with a surprising measure of detail. Adam was anesthetized—not by any artificial means, but God simply caused him to fall into a deep sleep. In such a slumber (especially in a world that was still a perfect paradise), Adam would feel no pain, of course. But, more significantly, the pure, passive restfulness of Adam's sleep makes an ideal illustration of how God's grace is *always* received. Grace is never set in motion by any effort or activity or volunteerism on our part, but it always flows freely from the sovereign will of God. Notice there's nothing to indicate that Adam *asked* God for a wife. Adam certainly wasn't given any conditions to fulfill as a prerequisite to receiving God's kindness. God Himself instigated this whole event and single-handedly brought it to pass—as an expression of sheer grace and benevolence to Adam. Adam was instrumental only in that he contributed a rib, but even that was done while he was asleep. The work was wholly and completely God's.

Adam's side was opened, a rib was carefully removed, and the incision was closed again. With such an infinitely skilled surgeon, and in the paradise of Eden prior to the curse, there was no danger of infection, none of the discomfort of postoperative pain, and (in all likelihood) not even a scar. God took a redundant bone that Adam would never miss and made for him the one thing he lacked: a soul mate. Adam lost a rib, but he gained a loving companion, created especially for him by the Giver of every good and perfect gift (James 1:17).

The Hebrew expression describing how God "made [the rib] into a woman" denotes careful construction and design. Literally, it means God *built* a woman. He carefully assembled a whole new creature with just the right set of attributes to make her the ideal mate for Adam.

Specially created by God for Adam from his own flesh and bone, Eve suited Adam perfectly in every way. She is a wonderful illustration of the goodness of God's grace and the perfect wisdom of His will. Again, God made her while Adam was asleep, without any tips or suggestions from him. Yet she perfectly met every need Adam had, satisfied every longing he may ever have felt, and delighted every faculty of his senses. She answered his need for companionship; she was a source of joy and gladness to him; and she made possible the procreation of the human race. She complemented Adam perfectly, and she enhanced everything about his existence. Eden was now truly a paradise.

When Adam awoke and found Eve, he must have been overjoyed!

The moment he saw her, he loved her. His first words upon meeting her express a profound sense of wonder, genuine delight, and abiding satisfaction: "This is now bone of my bones and flesh of my flesh." Clearly, he already felt a deep, personal attachment to Eve. She was a priceless treasure to be cherished, a worthy partner to encourage him, and a pleasing spouse who would love him in return. Instantly, he adored her and embraced her as his own.

The unique method of Eve's creation is deliberately emphasized, I think, in order to remind us of several crucial truths about womanhood in general.

First, it speaks of Eve's fundamental equality with Adam. The woman *(1)* was "taken out of man." They shared the same essential nature. She was not a different kind of creature; she was of exactly the same essence as Adam. She was in no way an inferior character made merely to serve him, but she was his spiritual counterpart, his intellectual coequal, and in every sense his perfect mate and companion.

Second, the way Eve was created reminds us of the essential unity that *(2)* is the ideal in every marriage relationship. Jesus referred to Eve's creation in Matthew 19:4–6 to prove that God's plan for marriage was established at the very beginning of human history and was based on the principles of monogamy, solidarity, and inviolability. "Have you not read that He who made them at the beginning 'made them male and female,' and said, 'For this reason a man shall leave his father and mother and be joined to his wife, and the two shall become one flesh'? So then, they are no longer two but one flesh. Therefore what God has joined together, let not man separate" (NKJV). So the one-flesh principle is perfectly illustrated in the method of Eve's creation. As a matter of fact, this is where that principle finds its true origin.

Third, the circumstances of Eve's creation illustrate how deep and *(3)* meaningful the marriage of husband and wife is designed to be. It is not *merely* a physical union, but a union of heart and soul as well. Eve was

Adam's complement in every sense, designed by God to be the ideal soul-companion for him. And the intimacy of her relationship with her husband derives from her being literally taken from his side. In his classic commentary on the Bible, Puritan author Matthew Henry wrote these familiar words, which have been adapted and quoted in many marriage ceremonies: "The woman was *made of a rib out of the side of Adam;* not made out of his head to rule over him, nor out of his feet to be trampled upon by him, but out of his side to be equal with him, under his arm to be protected, and near his heart to be beloved."

The symbolism Matthew Henry saw in Adam's rib accords well with what Scripture teaches about the proper relationship between husbands and wives. It reminds us, again, of how Scripture exalts women.

Fourth, Eve's creation contains some important biblical lessons about the divinely-designed role of women. Although Eve was spiritually and intellectually Adam's peer; although they were both of one essence and therefore equals in their standing before God and in their rank above the other creatures; there was nonetheless a clear distinction in their earthly roles. And this was by God's own deliberate creative design. In the words of the apostle Paul, "Man is not from woman, but woman from man. Nor was man created for the woman, but woman for the man" (1 Cor. 11:8–9 NKJV). Adam was created first; then Eve was made to fill a void in his existence. Adam was the head; Eve was his helper. Adam was designed to be a father, provider, protector, and leader. Eve was designed to be a mother, comforter, nurturer, and helper.

That God has ordained these different functions for men and women is clearly evident from nature alone (1 Cor. 11:14). Men and women do not possess equal physical strength. They are bodily and hormonally different (in a number of rather obvious ways). A mountain of empirical and clinical evidence strongly suggests that men and women are also dissimilar in several other important ways—including socially, emotionally, and psychologically.

6

To acknowledge that there are such fundamental differences between the genders, and that men and women were designed for different roles, may not correspond with modern feminist sensibilities, but this is, after all, what God's own Word says. God created men and women differently with a purpose, and His plan for them reflects their differences. Scripture is clear in teaching that wives should be subject to the authority of their husbands in marriage (Eph. 5:22–24; Col. 3:18; 1 Peter 3:1–6) and that women are to be under the authority and instruction of men in the church (1 Cor. 11:3–7; 14:34–35).

First Timothy 2:11–15 is a key passage on this issue, because that is where the apostle Paul defends the principle of male headship in the church. The *first* reason Paul gives for this arrangement stems from creation, not from the fall: "Adam was formed first, then Eve" (1 Tim. 2:13 NKJV). So the principle of male headship was designed into creation. It was not (as some have suggested) a consequence of Adam's sin and therefore something to be regarded as a fruit of evil. And when Scripture assigns men the role of headship in the church and in marriage, it reflects *God's blueprint as Creator.* I'm convinced that if people today would simply embrace God's purpose and seek to fulfill the roles God has designed for our respective genders, both men and women would be happier, the church would be healthier, and marriages would be stronger.

Adam was the representative head and archetype for the whole human race. But remember, although Eve was given a subordinate role, she remained Adam's spiritual and intellectual equal. She was his "helper," neither his supervisor nor his slave. By calling her Adam's "helper," Scripture stresses the mutuality and the complementary nature of the partnership. Eve was in no way inferior to her husband, but she was nonetheless given a role that was subordinate to his leadership.

Subordinate, yet equal? Yes. The relationships within the Trinity illustrate perfectly how headship and submission can function within a relationship of absolute equals. Christ is in no sense inferior to the Father. "In Him dwells all the fullness of the Godhead bodily" (Col. 2:9 NKJV). He has eternally existed "in the form of God . . . [and] equal with God" (Phil. 2:6 NKJV). "I and My Father are one," He testified (John 10:30 NKJV). The apostle John made it as clear as possible: From eternity past, Jesus was with God and was Himself God (John 1:1–2). Three divine Persons (Father, Son, and Holy Spirit) constitute the one true God of Scripture. All three are fully God and are fully equal. *Yet the Son is subordinate to the Father.* Jesus said, "I do not seek My own will but the will of the Father who sent Me" (John 5:30 NKJV). "I always do those things that please Him" (John 8:29 NKJV).

The apostle Paul drew a clear parallel between Jesus' willing submission to his Father and a wife's willing submission to her husband: "I want you to know that the head of every man is Christ, the head of woman is man, and the head of Christ is God" (1 Cor. 11:3 NKJV). So if you wonder how two persons who are truly equal can have a relationship where one is head and the other submits, you need look no further than the doctrine of the Trinity. God Himself is the pattern for such a relationship.

Eve's creation establishes a similar paradigm for the human race. Here is the sum of it: Men and women, though equal in essence, were designed for different roles. Women are in no sense intellectually or spiritually inferior to men, but they were quite clearly created for a distinctive purpose. In the economy of church and family, the Bible says women should be subordinate to the authority of men. Yet Scripture also recognizes that in a completely different sense, women are exalted *above* men—because they are the living and breathing manifestation of the glory of a race made in God's image (1 Cor. 11:7).

That was precisely Eve's position after creation and before the fall. She was under her husband's headship, yet she was in many ways an even more glorious creature than he, treasured and extolled by him. They were partners and companions, fellow-laborers in the garden. God dealt with Adam as head of the human race, and Eve was accountable to her husband. Far from consigning Eve to menial servitude or a state of domestic enslavement, this arrangement utterly liberated her.

This was true paradise, and Adam and Eve constituted a perfect microcosm of the human race as God designed it to be.

But then it was all ruined by sin. Tragically, Eve was the unwitting portal through which the tempter gained access to assault Adam.

HER TEMPTATION

Genesis 2 ends with a succinct description of the innocence of Eden's paradise: "They were both naked, the man and his wife, and were not ashamed" (v. 25 NKJV).

Genesis 3 then introduces the tempter, a serpent. This is clearly Satan, who has somehow manifested himself in the form of a reptile, though Scripture doesn't formally identify this creature as Satan until the final book of Revelation (Rev. 12:9; 20:2).

Satan was an angel who fell into sin. Isaiah 14:12–15 and Ezekiel 28:12–19 make reference to the demise of a magnificent angelic creature who is described as the highest and most glorious of all created beings. This can only be Satan. We're not told in Scripture precisely when Satan's fall occurred or what circumstances led to it. But it must have been sometime during the events described in Genesis 2, because at the end of Genesis 1, all creation—including everything in the visible universe as well as the spirit world—was complete, pristine, and unblemished. "God saw *everything* that He had made, and *indeed it was very good*" (Gen. 1:31 NKJV, emphasis added). But then in Genesis 3:1, we meet the serpent.

The chronology of the account seems to suggest that a very short time elapsed between the end of creation and the fall of Satan. A similarly short time appears to have elapsed between Satan's fall and Eve's temptation. It might have been only a few days—or perhaps even only a matter of hours. But it could not have been very long. Adam and Eve had not yet even conceived any children.

In fact, that is undoubtedly one of the main reasons the tempter wasted no time deceiving Eve and provoking her husband to sin. He wanted to strike at the head of the human race before the race had any opportunity to multiply. If he could beguile Eve and thereby cause Adam to fall at this moment, he could sabotage all of humanity in one deadly act of treason against God.

Here is the biblical account in full from Genesis 3:1–7:

> *Now the serpent was more cunning than any beast of the field which the LORD God had made. And he said to the woman, "Has God indeed said, 'You shall not eat of every tree of the garden?'"*
>
> *And the woman said to the serpent, "We may eat the fruit of the trees of the garden; but of the fruit of the tree which is in the midst of the garden, God has said, 'You shall not eat it, nor shall you touch it, lest you die.'"*
>
> *Then the serpent said to the woman, "You will not surely die. For God knows that in the day you eat of it your eyes will be opened, and you will be like God, knowing good and evil."*
>
> *So when the woman saw that the tree was good for food, that it was pleasant to the eyes, and a tree desirable to make one wise, she took of its fruit and ate. She also gave to her husband with her, and he ate. Then the eyes of both of them were opened, and they knew that they were naked; and they sewed fig leaves together and made themselves coverings.* (NKJV)

Satan came to Eve in disguise. That epitomizes the subtle way he intended to deceive her. He appears to have singled her out for this cunning deception when she was not in the company of Adam. As the weaker vessel, away from her husband, but close to the forbidden tree, she was in the most vulnerable position possible.

Notice that what the serpent told her was not only plausible; it was even partially true. Eating the fruit would indeed open her eyes to understand good and evil. In her innocence, Eve was susceptible to the devil's half-truths and lies.

The serpent's opening words in verse 1 set the tenor for all his deal-ings with humanity: "Has God indeed said . . . ?" Skepticism is implicit in the inquiry. This is his classic *modus operandi.* He questions the Word of God, suggesting uncertainty about the meaning of God's statements, raising doubt about the truthfulness of what God has said, insinuating suspicion about the motives behind God's secret purposes, or voicing apprehension about the wisdom of God's plan.

He twists the meaning of God's Word: "Has God indeed said, 'You shall not eat of every tree of the garden'?" God's commandment had actu-ally come to Adam as a positive statement: "Of every tree of the garden *you may freely eat*; but of the tree of the knowledge of good and evil you shall not eat" (Gen. 2:16–17 NKJV, emphasis added). The serpent casts the com-mand in negative language ("You shall *not* eat of every tree"), making God's expression of lavish generosity sound like stinginess. He was delibe-rately misrepresenting the character and the command of God.

It is likely that Eve had heard about God's only restriction not directly from God, but from her husband. Genesis 2:16–17 records that God gave the prohibition just prior to her creation, at a time when Adam must have been the lone recipient. This concurs perfectly with the biblical truth of Adam's position as the representative and head of the whole human race. God held him directly accountable. Eve's instruction and her protection were his responsibility as head of his family. Consequently, the farther she went from his side, the more she was exposed.

In the innocent bliss of Eden, of course, Eve was unaware that any danger like this existed. Even if (as it appears) the serpent discovered her looking at the tree, she was not thereby sinning. God had not forbidden the couple to *look* at the tree. Contrary to Eve's statement in Genesis 3:3,

God had not even forbidden them to *touch* the tree. She was exaggerating the rigors of God's one restriction.

Notice that she also understated the severity of God's warning, softening God's decisive tone of absolute certainty ("in the day that you eat of it you shall surely die" [Gen. 2:17 NKJV]) to the language of a mere potentiality ("lest you die" [Gen. 3:3 NKJV]).

At this point, however, it seems she was more flustered and confounded than anything else. There's no reason to assume she was purposely misrepresenting the facts. Perhaps for her protection, to put a fence around the danger, *Adam* had advised Eve not to "touch" the forbidden fruit. In any case, Eve was doing nothing wrong by simply looking at it. She would naturally have been curious. Satan seized the opportunity to beguile her, and thereby tempt Adam.

The second time the serpent speaks to Eve he does not merely misquote God's Word in order to put a sinister spin on it. This time he flatly contradicts what God had told Adam. God's word to Adam was, "In the day that you eat of it you shall surely die" (Gen. 2:17 NKJV). Satan's reply to Eve was the exact opposite: "You will not surely die" (3:4 NKJV).

Then Satan went on to confound Eve with his version of what would happen if she ate: "God knows that in the day you eat of it your eyes will be opened, and you will be like God, knowing good and evil" (v. 5 NKJV). This was another partial truth. If Eve ate, her eyes *would* be open to the knowledge of good and evil. In other words, she would forfeit her innocence.

But buried in the middle of those words is the lie of all lies. It is the same falsehood that still feeds the carnal pride of our fallen race and corrupts every human heart. This evil fiction has given birth to every false religion in human history. It is the same error that gave birth to the wickedness of Satan himself. This one lie therefore underlies a whole universe of evil: "You will be like God" (v. 5 NKJV).

Eating the fruit would *not* make Eve anything like God. It would (and did) make her like the devil—fallen, corrupt, and condemned.

But Eve was deceived. She "saw that the tree was good for food, that it was pleasant to the eyes, and a tree desirable to make one wise" (v. 6 NKJV). Notice the natural desires that contributed to Eve's confusion: her bodily appetites (it was good for food); her aesthetic sensibilities (it was pleasant to the eyes); and her intellectual curiosity (it was desirable for wisdom). Those are all good, legitimate, healthy urges—unless the object of desire is sinful, and then natural passion becomes evil lust. That can never result in any good. Thus we are told by the apostle John, "All that is in the world; the lust of the flesh, the lust of the eyes, and the pride of life; is not of the Father but is of the world" (1 John 2:16 NKJV).

Eve ate and then gave to her husband to eat. Scripture doesn't say whether Adam found Eve near the forbidden fruit or she went and found him. Either way, by Adam's act, according to Romans 5:12, "sin entered the world, and death through sin, and thus death spread to all men" (NKJV). That is known as the doctrine of original sin. It's one of the most important, truly foundational doctrines in Christian theology, and therefore certainly worth the effort to understand in the context of Eve's story.

People sometimes ask why it was *Adam's* failure that was so decisive for humanity and why Scripture treats Adam's disobedience as the means by which sin entered the world. After all, Eve actually ate the forbidden fruit first. She was the one who succumbed to the original temptation, allowed herself to be drawn away by an appeal to lust, and disobeyed God's command. Why is Adam's transgression deemed the original sin?

Remember, first of all, that 1 Timothy 2:14 says, "Adam was not deceived, but the woman being deceived, fell into transgression" (NKJV). Adam's sin was deliberate and willful in a way Eve's was not. Eve was deceived. But Adam chose to partake of the fruit Eve offered him with full knowledge that he was engaging in deliberate rebellion against God.

There is, however, an even more important reason why Adam's sin, rather than Eve's, led to the fall of all humanity. Because of Adam's unique position as head of the original family and therefore captain of the whole human race, Adam's headship had particular significance for all of humanity. God dealt with him as a kind of legal delegate for himself, his wife, and all their offspring. When Adam sinned, he sinned as our representative before God. When he fell, we fell with him. That is precisely why Scripture teaches that we are *born* sinful (see Gen. 8:21; Ps. 51:5; 58:3) and that we all share in *Adam's* guilt and condemnation (Rom. 5:18).

In other words, contrary to what many people assume, we don't fall from a state of complete innocence into sin individually, on our own. But Adam, who in effect was acting as an agent and proxy for the entire human race, plunged *all of humanity at once* into sin. In the words of Romans 5:19, "By one man's disobedience many were made sinners" (NKJV). Every one of Adam's progeny was condemned by his actions. And that is why the whole human race is said to be guilty because of what *he* did, and not because of what Eve did.

It is impossible to make sense of the doctrine of original sin if we ignore this principle of Adam's headship. Ultimately, it is impossible to make sense of Scripture at all without understanding this vital principle. In an absolutely crucial sense, even the truth of the gospel hinges on this very same idea of representative headship. Scripture says that Adam's headship over the human race is an exact parallel of Christ's headship over the redeemed race (Rom. 5:18; 1 Cor. 15:22). In the same way that Adam brought guilt on us as our representative, Christ took away that guilt for His people by becoming their head and representative. He stood as their proxy before the bar of divine justice and paid the price of their guilt before God. Jesus also did everything Adam failed to do, rendering obedience to God on behalf of His people. Therefore, "by one Man's obedience many will be made righteous" (Rom. 5:19 NKJV). In other words, Christ's righteousness counts as ours, because He took His place as the representative Head of all who trust Him. That is the gospel in a nutshell.

Don't get the idea, however, that Eve's sin was excusable because it wasn't as deliberate or as far-reaching as Adam's. Eve's sin was exceedingly sinful, and her actions demonstrated that she was a full and willing part-ner with Adam in his disobedience. (Incidentally, in a similar way, we all demonstrate by our own willful deeds that the doctrine of original sin is perfectly just and reasonable. No one can legitimately cast off the guilt of the human race by protesting that it is unfair for the rest of us to be tainted with guilt for Adam's behavior. Our own sins prove our com-plicity with him.)

Eve's sin subjected her to God's displeasure. She forfeited the paradise of Eden and inherited a life of pain and frustration instead. The divine curse against sin targeted her in a particular way.

HER HUMILIATION

The serpent was right about one thing: eating the forbidden fruit opened Eve's eyes so that she knew good and evil. Unfortunately, she knew evil by experiencing it—by becoming a willing participant in sin. And in a moment, her innocence was gone. The result was agonizing shame.

Scripture describes it in a few picturesque words: "Then the eyes of both of them were opened, and they knew that they were naked; and they sewed fig leaves together and made themselves coverings" (Gen. 3:7 NKJV).

Their famous attempt to make clothing of fig leaves perfectly illus-trates the utter inadequacy of every human device ever conceived to try to cover shame. Human religion, philanthropy, education, self-betterment, self-esteem, and all other attempts at human goodness ultimately fail to provide adequate camouflage for the disgrace and shame of our fallen state. All the man-made remedies combined are no more effective for removing the dishonor of our sin than our first parents' attempts to con-ceal their nakedness with fig leaves. That's because masking over shame doesn't really deal with the problem of guilt before God. Worst of all, a full atonement for guilt is far outside the possibility of fallen men and women to provide for themselves.

That was the realization Adam and Eve awoke to when their eyes were opened to the knowledge of good and evil. The Lord, of course, knew all about Adam's sin before it even occurred. There was no possibility of hiding the truth from Him, and He certainly did not have to come physically to the garden to find out what the first couple were up to. But Genesis tells the story from an earthly and human perspective. What we read in Genesis 3:8–13, in essence, is what Eve heard and saw:

> *And they heard the sound of the* LORD *God walking in the garden in the cool of the day, and Adam and his wife hid themselves from the presence of the* LORD *God among the trees of the garden.*
>
> *Then the* LORD *God called to Adam and said to him, "Where are you?"*
>
> *So he said, "I heard Your voice in the garden, and I was afraid because I was naked; and I hid myself."*
>
> *And He said, "Who told you that you were naked? Have you eaten from the tree of which I commanded you that you should not eat?"*
>
> *Then the man said, "The woman whom You gave to be with me, she gave me of the tree, and I ate."*
>
> *And the* LORD *God said to the woman, "What is this you have done?"* (NKJV)

It is evident that the shame of our first parents was accompanied by a deep sense of fear, dread, and horror at the prospect of giving account to God for what they had done. That is why they tried to hide. Like the fig leaves, their hiding place was inadequate to conceal them from the all-seeing eye of God.

Adam's reply reflects his fear, as well as a note of deep sorrow. But there's no confession. Adam seems to have realized that it was pointless to try to plead innocence, but neither did he make a full confession. What he did was try to pass off the blame. He immediately pointed the finger at the one closest to him: Eve.

Also implicit in Adam's words ("The woman whom *You* gave") was an accusation against God. So quickly did sin corrupt Adam's mind that in his blame shifting, he did not shy away from making God Himself an accessory to the crime. This is so typical of sinners seeking to exonerate themselves that the New Testament epistle of James expressly instructs us, "Let no one say when he is tempted, 'I am tempted by God'; for God cannot be tempted by evil, nor does He Himself tempt anyone. But each one is tempted when he is drawn away by his own desires and enticed" (James 1:13–14 NKJV). Adam, however, was subtly trying to put at least some of the blame on God himself.

But Adam handed most of the culpability to Eve. The Lord responded, not by arguing with Adam about it, but by turning to Eve and confronting her directly. Obviously, this was not a signal that Adam was off the hook. Rather, the Lord was giving Eve an opportunity to confess her part.

But she just tried to push the blame off onto the serpent: "The woman said, 'The serpent deceived me, and I ate'" (Gen. 3:13 NKJV). That was true enough (1 Tim. 2:14), but the serpent's guilt did not justify her sin. Again, James 1:14 stands as a reminder that whenever we sin, it is because we are drawn away by *our own lust*. No matter what means Satan may use to beguile us into sin—no matter how subtle his cunning—the responsibility for the deed itself still lies with the sinner and no one else. Eve could not escape accountability for what she had done by transferring the blame.

Notice, however, that the Lord made no argument and entertained no further dialogue. There was enough to condemn Adam and Eve in their own words, despite their efforts to avoid a full confession. All their excuses were no better at concealing their guilt than the fig leaves had been.

So in Genesis 3:14–19, the Lord simply pronounces a comprehensive curse that addresses the guilty parties in turn—first the serpent, then Eve, and finally Adam:

> So the LORD God said to the serpent: *"Because you have done this, you are cursed more than all cattle, and more than every beast of the field; on your belly you shall go, and you shall eat dust all the days of your life. And I will put enmity between you and the woman, and between your seed and her Seed; He shall bruise your head, and you shall bruise His heel."*
>
> To the woman He said: *"I will greatly multiply your sorrow and your conception; in pain you shall bring forth children; your desire shall be for your husband, and he shall rule over you."*
>
> Then to Adam He said, *"Because you have heeded the voice of your wife, and have eaten from the tree of which I commanded you, saying, 'You shall not eat of it': cursed is the ground for your sake; in toil you shall eat of it all the days of your life. Both thorns and thistles it shall bring forth for you, and you shall eat the herb of the field. In the sweat of your face you shall eat bread till you return to the ground, for out of it you were taken; for dust you are, and to dust you shall return."* (NKJV)

To examine the entire curse exhaustively might consume many chapters. It would certainly require more space than would be reasonable for a chapter like this. What we are chiefly interested in, of course, is how this curse relates to Eve in particular. Notice that the curse has three sections. The first part is addressed to the serpent; the second part to Eve; and the third part to Adam. But all three sections had serious ramifications for Eve. In order to see this clearly, let's start with the final section, which is addressed to Adam, and work our way backward.

Bear in mind, first of all, that the curse on Adam applied not only to him personally, but also to the entire human race. It furthermore promised significant changes in the earthly environment. So the curse on Adam had immediate and automatic implications for Eve (and for all their offspring) also. The loss of paradise and the sudden change in all of nature meant that Eve's daily life would be filled with onerous consequences, just as Adam's life would be. Her toil, like his, would become a burden. The sweat, the thorns and thistles, and ultimately the reality of death would all be part of her lot in life too. So the curse on Adam was a curse on Eve as well.

It is significant, I think, that the shortest section of the curse is the part dealing with Eve directly. Eve's part is completely contained in one verse of Scripture (v. 16), and it has two elements. One direct consequence of Eve's sin would be a multiplication of the pain and sorrow associated with childbirth. The other would be a struggle that would occur in her relationship with her husband. In other words, when the curse addresses Eve in particular, it deals with the two most important relationships in which a woman might naturally seek her highest joy: her husband and her children.

The first part of verse 16 is simple and straightforward: "I will greatly multiply your sorrow and your conception; in pain you shall bring forth children." Of course, sin is what brought sorrow and misery into the world in the first place. The expression *multiply your sorrow* does not suggest that there would have been a lesser degree of anguish or distress in an uncursed Eden anyway. Presumably, even childbirth would have been as painless and as perfect as every other aspect of Paradise. But this language simply recognizes that now, in a fallen world, sadness, pain, and physical difficulties would be part and parcel of the woman's daily routine. And in *childbirth*, the pain and sorrow would be "greatly multiplied"—significantly increased over the normal woes of everyday life. The bearing of children, which originally had the potential to bring the most undiluted kind of joy and gladness, would instead be marred by severe pain and difficulty.

The second part of the verse is a little harder to interpret: "Your desire shall be for your husband, and he shall rule over you." Clear light is shed on the meaning of that expression by a comparison with Genesis 4:7,

19

which uses exactly the same language and grammatical construction to describe the struggle we wage with sin: "Sin lies at the door. And its desire is for you, but you should rule over it" (NKJV). In other words, sin desires to gain mastery over you, but you need to prevail over it instead.

Genesis 3:16, using the very same language, describes a similar struggle that would take place between Eve and her husband. Before Adam sinned, his leadership was always perfectly wise and loving and tender. Before Eve sinned, her submission was the perfect model of meekness and modesty. But sin changed all of that. She would now chafe under his headship and desire to gain dominance over him. His tendency would be to suppress her in a harsh or domineering way. And thus we see that tensions over gender roles go all the way back to our first parents. It is one of the immediate effects of sin and the awful curse that it brought upon our race.

Paradise was utterly ruined by sin, and the severity of the curse must have shattered Eve's heart. But God's judgment against her was not entirely harsh and hopeless. There was a good deal of grace, even in the curse. To the eyes of faith, there were rays of hope that shone even through the cloud of God's displeasure.

For example, Eve might have been made subject to the serpent to whom she had foolishly acquiesced. But instead, she remained under the headship of her husband, who loved her. She might have been utterly destroyed, or made to wander alone in a world where survival would have been difficult. Instead, she was permitted to remain with Adam, who would continue to care for her and provide for her. Although their relationship would now have tensions that did not exist in Eden, she remained Adam's partner. Even though she might have justly been made an outcast and a pariah, she retained her role as a wife.

In the worst case, Eve might have even been forbidden to bear children. Instead, although the experience would now be painful and accompanied by sorrow, Eve would still be the mother of all living. In fact, her very name, given to her by Adam after the pronouncement of the curse, gave testimony to that fact. "Adam called his wife's name Eve; because she was the mother of all living" (Gen. 3:20 NKJV).

As a matter of fact, the promise that Eve would still bear children mitigated every other aspect of the curse. That one simple expectation contained a ray of hope for the whole human race. There was a hint in the curse itself that one of Eve's own offspring would ultimately over- *Christ* throw evil and dispel all the darkness of sin. Eve had set a whole world of evil in motion by her disobedience; now, through her offspring, she would produce a Savior. This powerful hope had *already* been implicitly given to her, in the portion of the curse where the Lord addressed the serpent.

HER EXPECTATION

God's curse on the serpent was the most severe of all. In the most literal and obvious sense, the curse appears to be addressed to the actual reptile. But remember, *this* reptile was somehow indwelt or controlled by Satan. The true significance of the curse, therefore, actually looks beyond the snake and his species. Its primary message is a grim sentence of condemnation against Satan himself.

Still, the curse *does* have important implications for the literal serpent and his species. Don't miss the fact that the Lord implicitly declares "all cattle, and . . . every beast of the field" accursed (Gen. 3:14 NKJV). Of course, God did not hold the animal kingdom culpable for Adam's sin. (Scripture never portrays animals as morally sentient beings, and this is no exception. Even in the case of the serpent, the moral fault lay in the satanic spirit who used the reptile's form, and not in the beast itself.) But God cursed even the animals for Adam's sin. In other words, the curse on them was part of God's judgment against Adam.

Remember, the curse had negative ramifications for Adam's whole environment. Evil is infectious, and, therefore, when Adam sinned, his entire domain was tainted. The sweeping extent of the curse reflects that truth. That is why, in verse 17, the Lord cursed even the ground. Obviously, the animal kingdom would be likewise subject to the many and far-reaching effects of Adam's rebellion. Every beast of the field would henceforth live in a decaying and dying world. They, too, would be subject to disease, destruction, disaster, death, and various other hardships that all stemmed from the presence of evil. Therefore the animals were also formally included in God's curse. They were consigned to suffer the miseries of evil that Adam's sin had brought into his environment. This was all part of *Adam's* judgment, a constant reminder to him about God's displeasure over sin.

But the serpent would be cursed above all species, reduced to crawling on his belly in the dust. This seems to suggest that serpents originally had legs. We're not given a physical description of the serpent prior to the curse, but it could well have been a magnificent and sophisticated creature. From now on, however, all serpents would be demoted to the dirt, condemned to writhe on the ground, and therefore unable to avoid eating the offscouring of all kinds of filth along with their food. Whatever the glories of this creature prior to the fall, he now would take a form that signified the loathsomeness of the tempter who indwelt him.

Furthermore, the serpent would forever bear the stigma of human contempt. The very real effects of this pronouncement are clearly evident in the human species' near-universal hatred of snakes. No other creature arouses so much fear and loathing.

But again, the full meaning of this text really looks beyond the reptile and addresses the satanic spirit who controlled him. The serpent's degradation to the dust simply mirrors and illustrates Satan's own demotion from heaven. "How you are fallen from heaven, O Lucifer, son of the morning! How you are cut down to the ground" (Isa. 14:12 NKJV). The loathing of all humanity likewise applies to Satan. Although our race is fallen and spiritually aligned with Satan against God (John 8:44), the devil himself is a reproach and a disgrace among Eve's children. People, as a rule, are naturally repulsed by Satan and satanic imagery.

But that's not all this means. The important spiritual implications of the curse against the serpent are even more profound than that. And I believe Eve understood this in some measure. Genesis 3:15 is often referred to as the *Protevangelium* (meaning, literally, "the first gospel"). Here is the earliest glimmer of good news for fallen humanity, and it comes in the opening words of God's *curse!* He says to the evil spirit indwelling the snake: "I will put enmity . . . between your seed and her Seed; He shall bruise your head, and you shall bruise His heel" (NKJV).

Though framed as a malediction against the tempter, that part of the curse was a bright ray of light for Eve. Here was an explicit promise that her Seed would bruise the evil one's head. She could not possibly have grasped the full scope of the divine pledge concealed in those words, but she could hardly have failed to take heart from what she heard.

First of all, the mere mention of "her Seed" indicated that she would bear children and have the opportunity to raise a family. At the very least, she now *knew* she was not going to be instantly and abruptly destroyed because of her sin. She would not be consigned to unmitigated condemnation alongside the serpent. Instead (and Eve surely understood that this was only owing to God's great grace and mercy), she would still have the opportunity to become the mother of the human race. Moreover, God would ensure that enmity would perpetually exist between Eve's descendents and that evil creature. All of this was clearly good news from Eve's perspective.

Even better, however, was the promise that her seed would bruise the serpent's head. This was a guarantee that her race would not be hopelessly subordinated to the evil one's domination forever. In fact, whether Eve fully grasped it or not, this curse against the serpent hinted at an ultimate remedy for her sin, giving Eve reason to hope that someday one of her descendants would inflict a crushing blow to the tempter's head, utterly and finally destroying the diabolical being and all his influence—and, in effect, overturning all the wickedness Eve had helped to unleash.

Make no mistake; that is precisely what these words meant. The curse against the serpent held a promise for Eve. Her "Seed" would crush the serpent's head. Her own offspring would destroy the destroyer.

This sense of Genesis 3:15 reflects the true divine intention. And that fact is made absolutely clear by the rest of Scripture. (Indeed, it is the main plot of the story the rest of Scripture tells.) For example, there is an echo of this same language in Romans 16:20: "The God of peace will crush Satan under your feet shortly" (NKJV). Hebrews 2:14 says Christ (who, of course, *is* the eternal "God of peace") took on human form—literally became one of Eve's offspring—so "that through death He might destroy him who had the power of death, that is, the devil" (NKJV). First John 3:8 says, "For this purpose the Son of God was manifested, that He might destroy the works of the devil" (NKJV). Thus Christ, who was uniquely "born of a woman" (Gal. 4:4 NKJV)—the offspring of a virgin, and God in human form—literally fulfilled this promise that the Seed of the woman would break the serpent's head.

How much of this did Eve genuinely understand? Scripture does not say, but it seems clear that Eve clung to the hope that eventually one of her own offspring would wound her mortal enemy. To borrow words from a slightly different context, she seemed to sense that her species would, by God's grace, be "saved in childbearing" (1 Tim. 2:15 NKJV). We can be certain that her deep enmity toward the tempter never wavered as long as she lived. She must have longed for the day when one of her children would smash his head.

Evidence of that hope is seen in her great joy upon first becoming a mother. Genesis 4:1 describes the birth of Cain, Eve's eldest son. Eve said, "I have acquired a man from the LORD" (NKJV). The Hebrew expression might literally be translated, "I have acquired a man; YHWH." Some commentators have suggested that perhaps she thought Cain was

God incarnate, the promised Redeemer. Scripture gives us few reasons to think her messianic hope was quite that highly developed. Certainly, if she even assumed Cain would be the promised Seed, she was sorely disappointed. He crushed his mother's heart rather than the serpent's head, by murdering Abel, his younger brother.

Whatever Eve may have meant by that expression in Genesis 4:1, it was nonetheless a clear expression of hope and rejoicing because of God's grace, compassion, kindness, and forgiveness toward her. There's a tone of exultation in it: "I have acquired a man from the LORD."

It is also clear that her hope was personified in her own children. She saw them as tokens of God's goodness and reminders of the promise that her seed would be the instrument by which the tempter's ultimate destruction was accomplished. In fact, when Eve bore Seth—after Cain had already broken her heart by murdering Abel—Scripture says, she "named him Seth [meaning, "appointed one"], 'For God has appointed another seed for me instead of Abel, whom Cain killed'" (Gen. 4:25 NKJV). The reference to the "appointed seed" *does* suggest that her heart had laid hold of the promise concealed in the curse, and she treasured the undying hope that one day her own Seed would fulfill that promise.

Were Adam and Eve saved? I believe they were. God's grace to them is exemplified in the way He "made tunics of skin, and clothed them" (Gen. 3:21 NKJV). In order for Him to do that, some animals had to be slain. Thus the first ever blood sacrifice was made by the hand of God on their behalf. Furthermore, concealed in God's declaration that the woman's Seed would defeat the serpent was an implicit promise that their sin and all its consequences would one day be vanquished and the guilt of it would be eradicated. We know from a New Testament perspective that this promise involved the sending of God's own Son to undo what Adam's sin did.

They believed that promise, insofar as they understood it. Scripture records that Seth founded a line of godly people: "As for Seth, to him also

25

a son was born; and he named him Enosh. Then men began to call on the name of the LORD" (Gen. 4:26 NKJV). Where would their knowledge of the Lord have come from? Obviously, it came from Adam and Eve, who had more direct and firsthand knowledge of God than anyone else since the fall. This godly line (which endures in the faith of millions even today) was to a large degree their legacy. Happily for Eve, it will eventually prove to be an infinitely more enduring legacy than her sin. After all, heaven will be filled with her redeemed offspring, and they will be eternally occupied with a celebration of the work of her Seed.

2
Sarah: Hoping Against Hope

❧

By faith Sarah herself also received strength to conceive seed, and she bore a child when she was past the age, because she judged Him faithful who had promised.

Hebrews 11:11 NKJV

Let's be honest: there are times in the biblical account when Sarah comes off as a bit of a shrew. She was the wife of the great patriarch Abraham, so we tend to think of her with a degree of dignity and honor. But reading the biblical account of her life, it is impossible not to notice that she sometimes behaved badly. She could throw fits and tantrums. She knew how to be manipulative. And she was even known to get mean. At one time or another, she exemplified almost every trait associated with the typical caricature of a churlish woman. She could be impatient, temperamental, conniving, cantankerous, cruel, flighty, pouty, jealous, erratic, unreasonable, a whiner, a complainer, or a nag. By no means was she always the perfect model of godly grace and meekness.

In fact, there are hints that she may have been something of a pampered beauty; a classic prima donna. The name given to her at birth, *Sarai*, means "my princess." (Her name was not changed to *Sarah* until she was ninety years old, according to Genesis 17:15.) Scripture remarks repeatedly about how stunningly attractive she was. Wherever she went, she instantly received favor and privilege because of her good looks. That kind of thing can spoil the best of women.

By the way, the biblical account of Sarah's life doesn't really even begin until she was already sixty-five years old. Amazingly, even at that age, her physical beauty was so remarkable that Abraham regularly assumed other powerful men would want her for their harems. And he was right. First a pharaoh, then a king, not realizing she was Abraham's wife, had designs on obtaining her as a wife. To this day, Sarah is remembered for her legendary beauty. A famous Moslem tradition teaches that Sarah resembled Eve. (That is especially significant in light of another Moslem tradition, which says Allah gave Eve two-thirds of all beauty, and then divided what remained of beauty among all other women.) But it's not necessary to embellish Sarah's glamour with fables. From the biblical account alone, it is clear that she was an extraordinarily beautiful woman.

From the time she became Abraham's wife, Sarah desired one thing above all others, and that was to have children. But she was barren throughout her normal childbearing years. In fact, that is practically the first thing Scripture mentions about her. After recording that Abraham took her as a wife in Genesis 11:29, verse 30 says, "But Sarai was barren; she had no child" (NKJV).

She was obviously tortured by her childlessness. Every recorded episode of ill temper or strife in her household was related to her frustrations about her own barrenness. It ate at her. She spent years in the grip of frustration and depression because of it. She desperately wanted to be a mother, but she finally concluded that God Himself was restraining her from having children (Gen. 16:2). So badly did she want her husband to have an heir that she concocted a scheme that was immoral, unrighteous, and utterly foolish. She rashly persuaded Abraham to father a child by her own housemaid.

Predictably, the consequences of such a carnal ploy nearly tore her life apart and seemed to leave a lasting scar on her personality. Her bitterness seethed for thirteen years, and she finally insisted that Abraham throw the other woman out, along with the child he had fathered by her.

Sarah's faults are obvious enough. She was certainly fallen. Her faith, at times, grew weak. Her own heart sometimes led her astray. Those shortcomings were conspicuous and undeniable. If those things were all we knew about Sarah, we might be tempted to picture her as something of a battle-ax—a harsh, severe woman, relentlessly self-centered and temperamental. She wasn't always the kind of person who naturally evokes our sympathy and understanding.

Fortunately, there was much more to Sarah than that. She had important strengths as well as glaring weaknesses. Scripture actually commends her for her faith and steadfastness. The apostle Peter pointed to her as the very model of how every wife should submit to her husband's headship. Although there were those terrible flashes of petulance and even cruelty (reminders that Sarah was an embattled, fleshly creature like us), Sarah's life on the whole is actually characterized by humility, meekness, hospitality, faithfulness, deep affection for her husband, sincere love toward God, and hope that never died.

A study in contrasts and contradictions, Sarah was indeed one extraordinary woman. Although she gave birth to only one son and didn't become a mother at all until she was well past the normal age of fertility, she is the principal matriarch in Hebrew history. Although her enduring faithfulness to her husband was one of the most exemplary aspects of her character, the most notorious blunder of her life involved an act of gross *un*faithfulness. She sometimes vacillated, but she ultimately persevered against unbelievable obstacles, and the steadfastness of her faith became the central feature of her legacy. In fact, the New Testament enshrines her in the Hall of Faith: "because she judged Him faithful who had promised" (Heb. 11:11 NKJV).

The full spectacle of Sarah's amazing faith doesn't really become apparent until we contemplate the many seemingly insurmountable obstacles to that faith.

HER BACKGROUND IN UR OF THE CHALDEANS

Sarah was half-sister to her husband, Abraham. In Genesis 20:12, Abraham describes for King Abimelech his relationship with his wife: "She is truly my sister. She is the daughter of my father, but not the daughter of my mother; and she became my wife" (NKJV). Terah was father to both of them, Sarah being ten years younger than Abraham (Gen. 17:17). We're not told the names of either of their mothers.

Incidentally, that kind of half-sibling marital relationship was not deemed incestuous in Abraham's time. Abraham's brother, Nahor, married a niece; and both Isaac and Jacob married cousins. Such marriages to close relatives were not the least bit unusual or scandalous in the patriarchal era—nor in previous times extending all the way back to creation. Obviously, since Adam and Eve were the only humans God originally created, it would have been absolutely essential in the beginning for some of Adam's offspring to wed their own siblings.

Scripture made no prohibition against consanguine marriages (matrimony between close relatives) until well after Abraham's time. No doubt one of the main reasons the Lord ultimately forbid the practice was because of the accumulation of genetic mutations in the human gene pool. When you begin with two genetically perfect creatures, there is no risk of any hereditary defects. Only gradually did the dangers associated with inbreeding arise. Therefore, no legal prohibition against incest even existed until the time of Moses. Then Leviticus 18:6–18 and 20:17–21 explicitly forbade several kinds of incest, including marriage between half-siblings. But the patriarchs should not be evaluated by laws that were only handed down many generations later. It was no sin for Abraham to take Sarah as his wife.

Scripture says virtually nothing about their early years of marriage. In fact, *all* we know about that era in their lives is the bitter truth that perpetually grated on Sarah's own consciousness: "Sarai was barren; she had no child" (Gen. 11:30 NKJV). That one statement sums up everything Scripture has to say about the first sixty-five years of Sarah's life! It is no wonder if she occasionally exhibited flashes of frustration and resentment.

Notice that the biblical account of Abraham's life likewise doesn't really begin until he was seventy-five. All we are told is that he had been born and raised in Sumeria, lower Mesopotamia, near the confluence of the Tigris and Euphrates rivers. (That's close to the head of the Persian Gulf in a region that is part of present-day Iraq.) Abraham's hometown was a famous urban center known as Ur of the Chaldeans.

Ur was the heart of a sophisticated pagan culture. Sarah and Abraham would have lived there during the very height of its power and affluence. The city government was a superstitious theocracy supposedly under the Babylonian moon god. (This was the same culture that built the famous ziggurats, those massive terraced towers upon which pagan temples were set.)

Abraham may have had some knowledge about the true God passed down to him by way of his ancestors. After all, Abraham was only a ninth-generation descendent from Shem, son of Noah. But having grown up in a pagan culture, Abraham was himself a pagan until the Lord called him out of Ur (Joshua 24:2).

It is obvious that the world cultures of Abraham's time were highly paganized. Going back even before the tower of Babel episode, love for the truth had obviously been in sharp decline for many generations. By the time Abraham came on the scene, idolatrous worship thoroughly dominated every world culture.

But there was still a scattered remnant of true believers. It is entirely likely that dispersed here and there among the world's population were faithful families who still knew and worshiped YHWH, having maintained their faith across the generations from Noah's time. For example, judging from details given in the book of Job, including the length of Job's lifespan, Job was probably a close contemporary of Abraham's. Job and his friends (lousy counselors though they were) had a thorough familiarity with the God of their ancestors. They lived in the land of Uz. The precise location of Uz is not certain, but it was clearly in the Middle East (Jer. 25:20)—yet not in the vicinity of Ur of the Chaldeans, where Abraham's family lived. So the remnant who still worshiped YHWH were not confined to any single location or limited to any one family.

In fact, in the biblical account of Abraham's life, we are also introduced to Melchizedek (Gen. 14:18). He represented an order of itinerant priests who knew the one true God and served Him. Abraham met Melchizedek somewhere in the Dead Sea region. Clearly, a few diverse remnants of faithful YHWH worship *did* still exist in Abraham's time.

The Lord's purpose in choosing and calling Abraham was to make him the father of a great nation that would be His witness to the world. That nation, Israel, would be formally covenanted with YHWH. Through them, the truth would be kept alive and preserved in perpetuity. Scripture says "the oracles of God" were committed to them (Rom. 3:2 NKJV). In other words, from the nation that came out of Abraham, prophets would arise. Through them the Scriptures would be given to the world. God would dwell in their midst and set His sanctuary among them. By their lineage a Deliverer, the Messiah, would arise. And in Him, all the nations of the world would be blessed (Gen. 18:18).

Sarah obviously had a key role to play in this plan. Abraham could never become the patriarch of a great nation if she did not first become mother to his offspring. She was surely aware of the Lord's promises to Abraham. She certainly would have longed to see those promises fulfilled. As long as she remained childless, however, the sense that everything somehow hinged on her must have pressed on her like a great burden on her shoulders.

HER JOURNEY TO THE LAND OF PROMISE

Apparently, while Abraham was still a young man living in Ur, the Lord spoke to him, saying, "Get out of your country, from your family and from your father's house, to a land that I will show you" (Gen. 12:1 NKJV).

Abraham obeyed, and Hebrews 11:8 expressly commends him for his obedience: "By faith Abraham obeyed when he was called to go out to the place which he would receive as an inheritance. And he went out, not knowing where he was going" (NKJV). But the journey was long and slow. It appears Abraham did not immediately separate from his family and his father's house. Instead, he took his father with him. Abraham may have been somewhat reluctant at first to sever the parental apron strings.

In fact, as Scripture recounts the first leg of the move from Ur of the Chaldeans, it appears that Abraham's father, Terah, was still acting as head of the extended family. "Terah took his son Abram and his grandson Lot, the son of Haran, and his daughter-in-law Sarai, his son Abram's wife, and they went out with them from Ur of the Chaldeans to go to the land of Canaan; and they came to Haran and dwelt there" (Gen. 11:31 NKJV). Clearly, Terah was still in charge. Scripture portrays him as the leader of the journey, with Abraham, Sarah, and Lot in tow.

But the first long leg of the journey stalled at Haran, about 650 miles northwest, roughly following the course of the Euphrates. Perhaps Terah was too old to travel anymore. We don't know how long Abraham and Sarah remained in Haran. But they did not get moving again until Terah died, and that was evidently some time. Scripture says Terah was more than two hundred years old when he died, and Abraham was seventy-five when he finally left Haran for the promised land.

That means Sarah was now sixty-five, the exact age most people today think is ideal for retirement. Sarah was by no means a *young* woman, even by the standards of the patriarchal era, when people obviously lived much longer and remained agile, healthy, and vigorous well past their sixties. The life of a nomad would be hard for anyone at sixty-five. And yet there is no sign whatsoever that she was reluctant or unwilling to go with Abraham to a land neither of them had ever seen.

In fact, what we know of Sarah suggests that far from complaining, she went eagerly, gladly, and enthusiastically with Abraham. She was utterly and completely devoted to her husband. Knowing that God wanted to make him the father of a great nation, she earnestly longed to give birth to the child who would set that whole process in motion.

Leaving Haran after burying his father, Abraham still had quite a large caravan. Scripture tells us, "Abram took Sarai his wife and Lot his brother's son, and all their possessions that they had gathered, and the people whom they had acquired in Haran, and they departed to go to the land of Canaan. So they came to the land of Canaan" (Gen. 12:5 NKJV).

That account suggests the final leg of the journey to Canaan was direct and uninterrupted. It was some 350 miles on foot (making the total journey from Ur more than a thousand miles). With a large caravan, moving a reasonable distance of eight to ten miles in a typical day, the trip from Haran to Canaan would have required only about six or seven weeks. Abraham seems not to have stopped until he reached Bethel, a fertile area with abundant springs.

Abraham's first act upon arrival there was the building of a stone altar. At that time, the Lord also appeared to Abraham. He expanded His original promises to Abraham, now adding that He would give all the surrounding land to Abraham's descendants. Although Abraham and Sarah remained nomads and vagabonds for the remainder of their days, this place and its altar remained their anchor. (This was also the very same place where Abraham's grandson Jacob would later be visited by YHWH and have that famous dream about a ladder that reached to heaven.)

But circumstances quickly forced Abraham to keep moving south.

"There was a famine in the land, and Abram went down to Egypt to dwell there, for the famine was severe in the land" (Gen. 12:10 NKJV). It was there, for the first time, that Abraham tried to pass Sarah off as his sister. He did this out of fear that if Pharaoh knew she was his wife, he would kill Abraham in order to have Sarah. Abraham's great faith wavered somewhat at this point. He succumbed to the fear of men. Had he simply trusted God, God would have protected Sarah (as He did in the end anyway).

But Scripture says that before they even entered Egypt, Abraham discussed with Sarah the dangers this place posed for a man with a beautiful wife. "When the Egyptians see you . . . they will say, 'This is his wife'; and they will kill me, but they will let you live," he told her (Gen. 12:12 NKJV). And so at Abraham's suggestion, she agreed to pose as his sister (v. 13). *Abraham's* motives were selfish and cowardly, and the scheme reflected a serious weakness in his faith. But Sarah's devotion to her husband is nonetheless commendable, and God honored her for it.

Stewards of Pharaoh saw her, pointed her out to Pharaoh, and brought her to his house. Scripture says Pharaoh showed favor to "brother" Abraham for Sarah's sake, lavishing him with livestock, apparently in anticipation of requesting her hand in marriage (v. 16). Meanwhile, by God's providence, Pharaoh did not violate her (v. 19). And to see that he did not, the Lord troubled Pharaoh's house with "great plagues" (v. 17 NKJV).

Somehow Pharaoh discovered the reason for the plagues, and he confronted Abraham with the deception, expelling the patriarch and his wife from Egypt (Gen. 12:19–20). Nonetheless, Pharaoh, preoccupied with more pressing things, did no harm to either of them, and when Abraham left Egypt, Pharaoh's favor toward Sarah had made Abraham a very wealthy man (Gen. 13:2). He and Sarah returned to Bethel, "to the place of the altar which he had made there at first. And there Abram called on the name of the LORD" (13:4 NKJV).

Henceforth, the Lord himself would be their dwelling place. Together, they "dwelt in the land of promise as in a foreign country, dwelling in tents . . . [while they] waited for the city which has foundations, whose builder and maker is God" (Heb. 11:9–10 NKJV). That is as good a summary as any of the earthly life Sarah inherited when she stepped out in faith to follow her husband: earthly inconvenience, mitigated by the promise of eternal blessing.

HER YEARNING FOR THE PROMISED BLESSING

Remember, Abraham and Sarah both came from an urban environment. They were not, as is commonly supposed, lifetime nomads or Bedouins who simply wandered all their lives because that is all they knew. Bear in mind that they did not *start* wandering until Abraham was already in his mid-seventies and Sarah was only a decade behind that. Life on the road was not something Sarah was accustomed to; it was something she had to learn to embrace.

What energized Sarah's willingness to leave all familiar surroundings, sever ties with her family, and commit to a life of rootless wandering?

Notice the nature of the vast promise God had made to Abraham: "I will make you a great nation; I will bless you and make your name great; and you shall be a blessing. I will bless those who bless you, and I will curse him who curses you; and in you all the families of the earth shall be blessed" (Gen. 12:2–3 NKJV). That is the first recorded hint of the Abrahamic Covenant, a formal pledge God made to Abraham and to his offspring forever. God's promise was unconditional and literally unlimited in the scope of its blessings. God would bless Abraham, make him a blessing, and make him a vehicle through which blessing would come to the whole world (Gal. 3:9–14). The promised blessing even had eternal implications.

In other words, redemption from sin and the means of salvation from divine judgment were part and parcel of the promise (Gal. 3:8, 16–17). Sarah understood that promise. According to Scripture, she believed it.

We know without question, from a New Testament perspective, that God's covenant with Abraham was an affirmation of the very same messianic promise God had already made to Eve in the garden when He declared that her seed would crush the head of the serpent. Just as Christ was the Seed of the woman who overthrows the serpent, He is also the Seed of Abraham by whom all the world will be blessed. Paul wrote, "Now to Abraham and his Seed were the promises made. He does not say, 'And to seeds,' as of many, but as of one, 'And to your Seed,' who is Christ" (Gal. 3:16 NKJV). This same promise is the central theme that extends all through Scripture, from Genesis 3 to its final fulfillment in the closing chapters of Revelation.

Abraham was the human channel through which the world would see the outpouring of God's redemptive plan. He understood that. Sarah understood and also embraced it. "She judged Him faithful who had promised" (Heb. 11:11 NKJV).

But despite her faith, she knew from a human perspective that her long years of childlessness already loomed large as a threat to the fulfillment of God's pledge. Sarah must have constantly pondered these things, and as time went by, the weight of her burden only increased.

Yet God kept giving her reasons to hope. In Genesis 15:7–21, YHWH restated and expanded His promise to Abraham, then formally ratified the covenant. It is significant that verse 12 says a deep sleep fell on Abraham; *then* the Lord single-handedly carried out the covenant ceremony. (Incidentally, the Hebrew word used in verse 12 is the same word describing the "deep sleep" that Adam fell into when the Lord took his rib to make Eve.) This detail about Abraham's sleep is given to stress the convenant was completely unconditional. The covenant was a unilateral promise from God to Abraham about what He, YHWH, would do. It made no demands of Abraham or Sarah whatsoever. It was a completely one-sided covenant.

If Sarah had simply realized that truth and embraced it, her whole burden would have been instantly lifted.

burden

HER FOOLISHNESS IN THE MATTER OF HAGAR

Instead, Sarah took it upon herself to hatch a scheme that was so ill-advised and so completely fleshly that she regretted it for the rest of her days. As a matter of fact, the evil consequences of that one act had unbelievably far-reaching implications. Frankly, some of the tensions we see in the Middle East today are rooted in Sarah's foolhardy ploy to try to concoct a man-made solution to her dilemma.

To be fair, from a purely human viewpoint, we can understand Sarah's despair. Ten more fruitless years passed after Abraham and Sarah arrived in Canaan (Gen. 16:3 NKJV). Sarah was now seventy-five years old, post-menopausal, and still childless. If God planned to make her the mother of Abraham's heir, why had He not done so by now? It was natural for her to think God was deliberately withholding children from her. As a matter of fact, He was. When *His* time came for the promise to be fulfilled, no one would be able to deny that this was indeed God's doing. His plan all along was for Sarah to have her first child in her old age, after every prospect of a natural fulfillment of the prophecy was exhausted and after every earthly reason for hope was completely dead. Thus YHWH would put His power on display.

But as she considered her circumstances, Sarah concluded that a kind of surrogate parenting was the only possible solution to her predicament. If God's promise to Abraham were ever going to be fulfilled, Abraham *had* to father children by some means. Sarah thus took it upon herself to try to engineer a fulfillment of the divine promise to Abraham. She unwittingly stepped into the role of God.

38

Sarah had a maidservant, named Hagar, whom she had acquired during their time in Egypt. Sarah apparently reasoned that since she owned Hagar, if Abraham fathered a child by Hagar, it would in effect be Sarah's child. "So Sarai said to Abram, 'See now, the LORD has restrained me from bearing children. Please, go in to my maid; perhaps I shall obtain children by her.' And Abram heeded the voice of Sarai" (16:2 NKJV).

This was the first recorded case of polygamy in Scripture involving a righteous man. The very first bigamist on biblical record was Lamech (Gen. 4:19). He was an evil descendant of Cain. (He is not to be confused with another Lamech, described in Genesis 5:25–29, who was Noah's father and who descended from the line of Seth.)

Abraham took a concubine, at his wife's urging. "Sarai, Abram's wife, took Hagar her maid, the Egyptian, and gave her to her husband Abram to be his wife" (Gen. 16:3 NKJV). This was a sorry precedent for the patriarch of the nation to set. In generations to come, Jacob would be duped by his uncle into marrying both Leah and Rachel (29:23–31); David would take concubines (2 Sam. 5:13); and Solomon would carry polygamy to an almost unbelievable extreme, maintaining a harem of more than a thousand women (1 Kings 11:1–3).

But God's design for marriage was monogamy from the beginning. "A man shall leave his father and mother and be joined to his wife, and *the two* shall become *one flesh*" (Matt. 19:4–5 NKJV, emphasis added). Paul likewise made clear what God's ideal for marriage is: "Let each man have *his own wife*, and let each woman have *her own husband*" (1 Cor. 7:2 NKJV, emphasis added). Disobedience to that standard has always resulted in evil consequences. David's polygamous heart led to his sin with Bathsheba. Solomon's marital philandering destroyed him and divided his kingdom (1 Kings 11:4). No good has ever come from any violation of the "one-flesh" principle of monogamy. Abraham's union with Hagar is certainly no exception.

As soon as Hagar conceived, Sarah *knew* it was a grave mistake. Hagar suddenly became haughty and contentious toward Sarah: "When she [Hagar] saw that she had conceived, her mistress [Sarah] became despised in her eyes" (Gen. 16:4 NKJV).

Here, then, is the first outburst of temper we see from Sarah: "Sarai said to Abram, 'My wrong be upon you! I gave my maid into your embrace; and when she saw that she had conceived, I became despised in her eyes. The LORD judge between you and me'" (Gen. 16:5 NKJV).

It is true that Sarah was being unreasonable. This whole sordid plan was, after all, her big idea. Yes, as the spiritual head of the household, Abraham should have rejected Sarah's plan out of hand—but it's still not quite fair to pin *all* the guilt on him. On the other hand, this fit of Sarah's was deliberately provoked by Hagar. Her insolent treatment of Sarah was utterly indefensible. No doubt, Hagar knew all too well about Sarah's extreme grief over her own barrenness. Now she was deliberately putting salt in Sarah's wound. Since Hagar was the servant and Sarah the one in charge, this was the most brazen kind of deliberate impudence.

A section of the book of Proverbs deals with precisely this situation:

> *Under three things the earth quakes,*
> *And under four, it cannot bear up:*
> *Under a slave when he becomes king,*
> *And a fool when he is satisfied with food,*
> *Under an unloved woman when she gets a husband,*
> *And a maidservant when she supplants her mistress.* (30:21–23 NASB)

The truth, however, is that every party in this whole affair was guilty, and all of them ended up reaping bitter fruit from what they had sown.

Abraham recognized the legitimacy of Sarah's complaint. He might have been wise to step in as an arbitrator and seek a solution that would have been fair to both women. But given Sarah's disposition at that moment, he did what most husbands would probably do and simply let

Sarah deal with Hagar her own way. "Abram said to Sarai, 'Indeed your maid is in your hand; do to her as you please.' And when Sarai dealt harshly with her, she fled from her presence" (Gen. 16:6 NKJV).

To understand Sarah's extreme frustration, let's follow Hagar for a moment. Notice first that although Sarah dealt harshly with her maidservant, the Lord showed extreme grace to Hagar. The Angel of the Lord sought her out. In all likelihood, this was no created angel, but a visible manifestation of YHWH himself in angelic or human form. (I'm inclined to think that this Angel was actually the preincarnate Son of God. We meet the same Angel several times in the Old Testament, including Genesis 22:11–18; Exodus 3:2–5; and 1 Kings 19:5–7.) Notice that He spoke to Hagar in the first person as YHWH, not in the third person, as an angelic messenger speaking on YHWH's behalf would do.

His words to Hagar were gentle and full of mercy. He first approached her by asking where she had come from and where she was going. He addressed her directly as "Hagar, Sarai's maid," however, both to make clear that he knew exactly who she was and to remind her of her duty. Then, to make this explicit, when Hagar answered truthfully, the Angel said, "Return to your mistress, and submit yourself under her hand" (Gen. 16:9 NKJV). As a legally indentured servant, she had no right to run away, and she needed to go back and be humbly obedient.

The Angel then made an amazing, completely unsolicited promise to Hagar: "I will multiply your descendants exceedingly, so that they shall not be counted for multitude" (Gen. 16:10 NKJV). Prophetically, he described her unborn son for her, saying she would call him Ishmael and that he would be wild, yet dwell in the presence of his brethren (16:12).

She, in return, acknowledged Him by a unique name: "El-Roi," or "the God who sees," a reference to the omniscient eye that followed her and sought her out even when she tried to hide (16:13 NKJV).

Consider this, however: Sarah had never received such a promise from God. Sarah's faith resided in promises God had made to Abraham. Up to this point, Sarah had never explicitly been named in the covenant God made with Abraham. God had already confirmed His promise to Abraham on no less than three major occasions. He first told Abraham he would be the father of a great nation (12:3). He then promised to make Abraham's seed as the dust of the earth—"so that if a man could number the dust of the earth, then your descendants also could be numbered" (13:16 NKJV). When Abraham later reminded the Lord that he still lacked a legitimate heir, God promised once again that Abraham's seed would be like the stars of the sky in number (15:1–6).

On none of those occasions had God ever expressly stated that Sarah would be matriarch to the nation in question. That was her hope and expectation. But what the episode with Hagar shows is that Sarah's hope was beginning to wane. She was slowly losing heart.

HER PERSEVERANCE THROUGH YEARS OF SILENCE

When Ishmael was born to Hagar, Scripture says Abraham was eighty-six years old (Gen. 16:16). Thirteen more frustrating years passed for Sarah after that. She remained barren. By that time she was eighty-nine years old. She had lived in Canaan for twenty-four years. Her husband was about to have his hundredth birthday. If her hope was not utterly shattered, it must have hung by a very thin thread.

Here's where the greatness of Sarah's faith shines through. She had harbored hope for so long. Year after year had come and gone. She was now an old woman, and no matter how often she and Abraham tried to conceive, the promise was *still* unfulfilled. Most women would have given up long before this. A lesser woman might have despaired of ever seeing YHWH's promise fulfilled and turned to paganism instead. But we are reminded again that Sarah "judged Him faithful who had promised" (Heb. 11:11 NKJV). This is what made her so extraordinary.

Finally, when Abraham was ninety-nine, the Lord appeared to him again and once more renewed the covenant. This was an especially important restatement of the covenant. The passage is long, and there's not enough space here to cover it in detail, but the Lord once again reiterated and expanded the vital promises he had made to Abraham. Every time the promises came, they got bigger: "My covenant is with you, and you shall be a father of many nations" (Gen. 17:4 NKJV). Not just "a great nation"; not merely descendants as numerous as the stars or the dust; but "many nations." To this aged man who had managed to father only one son (and that by less than honorable means), God said, "I will make you exceedingly fruitful; and I will make nations of you, and kings shall come from you" (17:6 NKJV).

It was also at this point that God gave Abraham his name, changing it from his birth name, Abram (17:5 NKJV). *Abram* means "exalted father"; *Abraham* means "father of many nations."

The Lord also formally extended the Abrahamic Covenant across the generations, making the whole land of Canaan "an everlasting possession" for Abraham's offspring forever (17:7–8 NKJV). Finally, God gave Abraham the sign of circumcision, with instructions for how it was to be administered (17:10–14). Circumcision became the sign and the formal seal of the covenant. Everything germane to the covenant was now in place.

Significantly, at the beginning of the chapter, YHWH revealed Himself to Abraham with a new name: "Almighty God," *El Shaddai* in Hebrew (17:1 NKJV). The name deliberately highlighted God's omnipotence. After hearing these promises so many times, Abraham might have been wondering whether he would ever see the son who embodied the fulfillment of the promises. The name was a subtle reminder to Abraham that nothing was too hard for God.

Having said all that, the Lord then turned the subject to Sarah. For the first time on record, He specifically brought Sarah by name into the covenant promises: "Then God said to Abraham, 'As for Sarai your wife, you shall not call her name Sarai ["my princess"], but Sarah ["Princess"] shall be her name. And I will bless her and also give you a son by her; then I will bless her, and she shall be a mother of nations; kings of peoples shall be from her'" (17:15–16 NKJV). By removing the possessive pronoun ("my"), the Lord was taking away the limiting aspect of her name, since she was to be ancestor to many nations.

There's no indication that Sarah was present to hear this; the context suggests that she was not. We can be certain she heard *about* it from Abraham at the first opportunity. Notice his reaction: "Then Abraham fell on his face and laughed, and said in his heart, 'Shall a child be born to a man who is one hundred years old? And shall Sarah, who is ninety years old, bear a child?'" (17:17 NKJV). There was probably as much relief and gladness in the laughter as there was incredulity. Surely we can understand Abraham's amazement, perhaps even tinged with a measure of uncertainty. But don't mistake it for unbelief. In Romans 4:20–21, the apostle Paul, speaking of this very moment, says Abraham "did not waver at the promise of God through unbelief, but was strengthened in faith, giving glory to God, and [was] fully convinced that what He had promised He was also able to perform" (NKJV).

Abraham also pleaded with God not to overlook Ishmael, at this point thirteen-years-old and no doubt beloved by his father: "Abraham said to God, 'Oh, that Ishmael might live before You!'" (Gen. 17:18 NKJV).

The Lord immediately reiterated the promise regarding Sarah: "No, Sarah your wife shall bear you a son, and you shall call his name Isaac; I will establish My covenant with him for an everlasting covenant, and with his descendants after him" (v. 19 NKJV). Sarah's son, not Hagar's, would be the child in whom the covenant promises would find their fulfillment (Gal. 4:22–28).

The Lord had one thing left to say: "And as for Ishmael, I have heard you. Behold, I have blessed him, and will make him fruitful, and will multiply him exceedingly. He shall beget twelve princes, and I will make him a great nation. But My covenant I will establish with Isaac, whom Sarah shall bear to you at this set time next year" (Gen. 17:20–21 NKJV). For the first time, here was a promise, with a fixed date, assuring Sarah of her place in the covenant. With that, the interview was over, and Scripture says simply that He "went up from Abraham" (v. 22 NKJV).

Abraham must have immediately found Sarah and reported to her all that the Lord said. Whatever her reaction, she certainly understood that *Abraham* believed the promise, because he immediately was circumcised, and he had every male in his household circumcised as well, whether they had been "born in the house or bought with money from a foreigner" (vv. 23–27 NKJV).

HER JOY IN THE FULFILLMENT OF THE PROMISE

The next time the Lord appeared to Abraham, one of His express purposes was to renew the promise for Sarah's sake so that she could hear it with her own ears. Genesis 18 describes how the Lord visited Abraham with two angels. Abraham saw them far off, and (perhaps even before he realized who they were) immediately had Sarah begin preparation of a meal for them. He promised them "a little water . . . [and] a morsel of bread," but he actually had a calf slain and gave them a feast (Gen. 18:4–8 NKJV). Sarah's willingness to entertain guests so elaborately on such short notice is one of the marks of her submission to Abraham mentioned by the apostle Peter when he held Sarah up as a model for wives. Peter wrote, "In this manner, in former times, the holy women who trusted in God also adorned themselves, being submissive to their own husbands, as Sarah obeyed Abraham, calling him lord" (1 Peter 3:5–6 NKJV). This was the very instance Peter had in mind. In fact, while Sarah is always portrayed as submissive to Abraham, Genesis 18:12 is the only place in the Old Testament record where she referred to him as "my lord" (NKJV).

While they were eating, the men asked, "Where is Sarah your wife?" (Gen. 18:9 NKJV).

"Here, in the tent," Abraham replied, establishing that he knew she was within earshot. Scripture describes the details of the conversation that followed:

> And He said, "I will certainly return to you according to the time of life, and behold, Sarah your wife shall have a son." (Sarah was listening in the tent door which was behind him.)
>
> Now Abraham and Sarah were old, well advanced in age; and Sarah had passed the age of childbearing. Therefore Sarah laughed within herself, saying, "After I have grown old, shall I have pleasure, my lord being old also?"
>
> And the LORD said to Abraham, "Why did Sarah laugh, saying, 'Shall I surely bear a child, since I am old?' Is anything too hard for the LORD? At the appointed time I will return to you, according to the time of life, and Sarah shall have a son."
>
> But Sarah denied it, saying, "I did not laugh," for she was afraid. And He said, "No, but you did laugh!" (Gen. 18:10–15 NKJV)

Sarah's laughter (just like Abraham's earlier) seems to have been an exclamation of joy and amazement rather than doubt. Yet when the Lord asked, "Why did Sarah laugh?" she denied it. That denial was motivated by fear. She was afraid because she had not laughed aloud, but "within herself." As soon as she realized this stranger had such a sure and thorough knowledge of her heart, she knew instantly and definitively that it was the Lord.

The year that followed was a difficult and busy year for Abraham and Sarah. That was the year God destroyed Sodom and Gomorrah (Gen. 18:16–19:29). And during that same year, Abraham journeyed south again, this time into the land ruled by Abimelech, king of Gerar. Sarah, though now ninety, was still beautiful enough to stir the passions of a king. What had happened in Egypt twenty-five years earlier was replayed once more. Abraham again tried to pass Sarah off as his sister, and Abimelech, smitten with her beauty, began to pursue her. But God spared Sarah, by warning Abimelech in a dream that she was Abraham's wife (Gen. 20:3). Scripture underscores the fact that Abimelech was not permitted by God to touch her (20:6), lest there be any question about whose child she would soon bear.

Abimelech, having been frightened when YHWH appeared to him in the dream, was gracious to Abraham and Sarah. He lavished gifts on Abraham and said, "See, my land is before you; dwell where it pleases you" (20:15 NKJV). To Sarah he said, "Behold, I have given your brother a thousand pieces of silver; behold, it is your vindication before all who are with you, and before all men you are cleared" (20:16 NASB).

Immediately after that incident, according to Scripture, "The LORD visited Sarah as He had said, and the LORD did for Sarah as He had spoken. For Sarah conceived and bore Abraham a son in his old age, at the set time of which God had spoken to him" (21:1–2 NKJV). Sarah named him Isaac, meaning "laughter." And Sarah said, "God has made me laugh, and all who hear will laugh with me" (21:6 NKJV). Thus she confessed the laugh she had previously tried to deny.

We're given a fascinating insight into Sarah's real character by the fact that she saw genuine humor in the way God had dealt with her. "Who would have said to Abraham that Sarah would nurse children? For I have borne him a son in his old age" (v. 7 NKJV). Despite her occasional bursts of temper and struggles with discouragement, Sarah remained an essentially good-humored woman. After those long years of bitter frustration, she could still appreciate the irony and relish the comedy of becoming a mother at such an old age. Her life's ambition was now realized, and the memory of years of bitter disappointment quickly disappeared from view. God had indeed been faithful.

HER HARSHNESS IN HER TREATMENT OF ISHMAEL

Sarah plays a major role in only one more episode recounted by Scripture.

Isaac was finally weaned—and from what we know of the culture, he would therefore have been a young toddler, probably two- or three-years-old. Scripture says, "Abraham made a great feast on the same day that Isaac was weaned" (21:8 NKJV). It was a time for celebration. But something happened that was the final straw for Sarah in her long struggle to accept Hagar as her husband's concubine. She saw Ishmael making fun of Isaac (v. 9). Scripture doesn't say *why* Ishmael was mocking. It was probably for some silly, childish reason. As any parent will attest, such behavior is by no means out of the ordinary for a child Ishmael's age. He was probably no older than fourteen at this point, just emerging from childhood into young manhood—old enough to be responsible for his behavior, but not old enough to be wise.

But it was too much for Sarah to endure. She immediately said, "Cast out this bondwoman and her son; for the son of this bondwoman shall not be heir with my son, namely with Isaac" (v. 10 NKJV).

For Abraham, all the joy instantly went out of the celebration. Ishmael was, after all, his firstborn son. He genuinely loved him. Remember Abraham's earlier plea to God, "Oh, that Ishmael might live before You!" (Gen. 17:18 NKJV).

Was Sarah really being overly harsh? In truth, she was not. Virtually any woman forced to share her husband with a concubine would respond to a situation like this exactly as Sarah did. She was Abraham's true wife. Hagar was an interloper. Besides, according to the promise of God Himself, Isaac was Abraham's true heir, promised by God to be the one through whom the covenant blessing would eventually see fulfillment. It confused things beyond measure for Ishmael to be in a position to claim the right of the firstborn over the one true heir appointed by God to succeed Abraham. Ishmael was a threat to God's purpose for Abraham's line as long as he remained in any position to claim that *he*, rather than Isaac, was Abraham's rightful heir.

So what may appear at first glance to be an extreme overreaction was actually another proof of Sarah's great faith in God's promise. God Himself affirmed the wisdom of her demand: "God said to Abraham, 'Do not let it be displeasing in your sight because of the lad or because of your bondwoman. Whatever Sarah has said to you, listen to her voice; for in Isaac your seed shall be called'" (21:12 NKJV).

Ishmael was by no means totally abandoned. The Lord promised to make a great nation of Ishmael too—"because he is your seed" (v. 13 NKJV). YHWH subsequently appeared to Ishmael and Hagar in their extremity and promised to meet all their needs (vv. 14–21). Furthermore, some kind of family tie was continually maintained between the lines of Ishmael and Isaac, because when Abraham died, both sons working together buried their father alongside Sarah (25:9–10).

The apostle Paul uses the expulsion of Hagar as an illustration of the conflict between law and grace. He calls it "an allegory" (Gal. 4:24 KJV), but we're not to think he is denying the historical facts of the Genesis account. Instead he is treating it as typology—or better yet, a living object lesson. Hagar, the bondwoman, represents the slavery of legalism (the bondage of trying to earn favor with God through works). Sarah, the faithful wife, represents the perfect liberty of grace. Paul was reminding the Galatian believers that "we, brethren, as Isaac was, are children of promise" (v. 28 NKJV)—saved by grace, not vainly hoping to be saved by works. "But, as he who was born according to the flesh then persecuted him who was born according to the Spirit, even so it is now" (v. 29 NKJV). Just as Ishmael taunted Isaac, so the false teachers in Galatia were persecuting true believers. Paul's conclusion? "Cast out the bondwoman and her son, for the son of the bondwoman shall not be heir with the son of the freewoman" (v. 30 NKJV). Harsh as it may have seemed, there was a very crucial, necessary, and positive spiritual principle in the expulsion of Hagar and Ishmael. This symbolized the important truth that the kind of religion that is dependent on human effort (symbolized by the carnal scheme that conceived Ishmael as an artificial fulfillment of God's promise) is utterly incompatible with divine grace (symbolized by Isaac, the true heir of God's promise). And the two are so hostile to one another that they cannot even abide in close proximity.

HER HAPPINESS IN HER WANING YEARS

After Hagar was cast out, Sarah returned to a healthy, monogamous life with her beloved husband and their child, Isaac, who was a perpetual reminder to both Sarah and Abraham of God's staunch faithfulness. As far as we know, the rest of her years were lived out in joy and peace.

Sarah doesn't even appear in the biblical account of Abraham's near sacrifice of Isaac. That whole event was uniquely meant as a test of *Abraham's* faith. Sarah seems to have been kept completely isolated from it until it was over. It occurred in the land of Moriah (Gen. 22:2). (In later generations, the city of Jerusalem surrounded the area known as Moriah, and Mount Moriah, at the heart of the city, was the precise spot where the Temple was situated, according to 2 Chronicles 3:1). Moriah was some forty-five miles from Beersheba, where Abraham was then residing (Gen. 21:33–34). In any event, Sarah's faith had already been well tested. She had long since demonstrated her absolute trust in God's promises. And the stamp of God's approval on her is contained in those New Testament passages that recognize her for her steadfast faithfulness.

In fact, in the very same way the New Testament portrays Abraham as the spiritual father of all who believe (Rom. 4:9–11; Gal. 3:7), Sarah is pictured as the spiritual matriarch and the ancient epitome of all faithful women (1 Peter 3:6. Far from isolating those memorable instances where Sarah behaved badly, it commemorates her as the very epitome of a woman adorned with "the incorruptible beauty of a gentle and quiet spirit" (1 Peter 3:4 NKJV).

That is a fitting epitaph for this truly extraordinary woman.

3

RAHAB: A HORRIBLE LIFE REDEEMED

❦

Salmon begot Boaz by Rahab, Boaz begot Obed by Ruth, Obed begot *establishing the lineage to Christ*
Jesse, and Jesse begot David the king.

Matthew 1:5–6 NKJV

hen Rahab first appears in the biblical account, she is one of the most unsavory characters imaginable. In fact, she is introduced as "a harlot named Rahab" (Josh. 2:1 NKJV). If you had met her before the great turning point of her life, you might have instantly written her off as completely hopeless. She was an immoral woman living in a pagan culture that was fanatically devoted to everything God hates. The culture itself was on the brink of judgment. Their long descent into the abyss of moral and spiritual corruption had been intentional, and now it was irreversible.

As far as we know, Rahab had always been a *willing* participant in her civilization's trademark debauchery. She had personally profited from the evil that permeated that whole society. Now that God had called for the complete destruction of the entire culture because of their extreme wickedness, why shouldn't Rahab also receive the just desserts of her own deliberate sin?

As far as the record of her life is concerned, there were no redeeming qualities whatsoever about Rahab's life up to this point. On the contrary, she would have been in the very *basement* of the moral hierarchy in a Gentile culture that was itself as thoroughly degenerate and as grossly pagan as any society in world history. She was a moral bottom-feeder. She made her living off that culture's insatiable appetite for unbridled debauchery, catering to the most debased appetites of the very dregs of society. It is hard to imagine a more unlikely candidate for divine honor than Rahab.

Yet in Hebrews 11:31 (though identified even there as "the harlot Rahab" [NKJV]), she is specifically singled out by name for the greatness of her faith, and she even appears in the genealogy of Christ in Matthew 1. Extraordinary? That word is an understatement in Rahab's case.

AN UNLIKELY BACKGROUND

Rahab lived in Jericho at the time of Joshua. Her house was not in some back alley of town, but perched right on the famous wall (Josh. 2:15). The wall must have been a wide affair, certainly spacious enough on top for buildings and either a walkway or a road. This was almost certainly a prime location in the high-rent business district. It is fair to assume, then, that Rahab had enjoyed phenomenal financial success in her trade.

Unfortunately, her "trade" was prostitution. She regularly sold herself to the most wicked men in that already-wicked city.

Jericho was part of the Amorite kingdom, a grotesquely violent, totally depraved, thoroughly pagan culture so hell-bent on the pursuit of everything evil that God Himself had condemned them and ordered the Israelites to wipe them from the face of the earth (Deut. 20:17). In fact, the Amorite culture had been so completely and maliciously corrupt for so long (going back at least to the time of Abraham), that their evil lifestyle was the very reason God had granted Abraham and his heirs rights to their land in the first place (Deut. 18:12; 1 Kings 21:26). The Lord had promised Abraham that his descendants would begin to possess the land as soon as the wickedness of the Amorites was complete (Gen. 15:16). That time had now come. This evil nation had reached God's maximum tolerance level.

Rahab therefore epitomized the vileness of the Amorite culture at a point when they had collectively filled the measure of human wickedness to its very brim. Her whole life had been devoted to the profane pursuit of carnal self-gratification. Her livelihood was totally dependent on consensual evil. She was enslaved to the most diabolical kinds of passion, in bondage to her own sin, and held captive by a monstrous society that was itself already under God's sentence of condemnation—indeed, marked out for *eternal* destruction. But divine grace redeemed her and liberated her from all of that, plucking her as a brand from the fire.

Here is the historical setting for Rahab's story: Moses had died (Josh. 1:1–2). The generation of Israelites who had come out of Egypt were all dead too. More than a million Israelites had originally left Egypt under Moses' leadership (Ex. 12:37). Because of that generation's collective stubbornness and persistent unbelief, when they first reached the very doorstep of the Promised Land at Kadesh-Barnea, everyone over twenty years of age was prohibited from entering. An entire generation was doomed to die in the wilderness without even seeing another glimpse of the Promised Land.

There were two significant exceptions (Num. 14:30): Joshua and Caleb. Those two men had scouted the Promised Land together for Moses. They had returned enthusiastic about the prospects of Israel's new homeland. They affirmed what God had said about the land. But when ten other spies returned with a conflicting report, discouraged, warning of the dangers that lay ahead, the people of Israel balked at entering the land. They listened to the unbelief of the pessimists rather than to the promise of YHWH. Then and there, the entire nation staged a mutiny against Moses

53

40 YRS. of wandering because of unbelief

and against God (Num. 13–14). That was the final straw. That is why Israel was made to wander for forty years. It was a divine judgment against them because of their unbelief (Num. 14:30–35). In the end, the carcasses of that whole generation (except the two faithful men) were buried in scattered graves in the wilderness, where the harsh elements eventually consumed them (vv. 32–33).

Thirty-eight years had now passed since that rebellion at Kadesh-Barnea. The book of Joshua starts with the Israelites situated again on the doorstep of Canaan—this time near Acacia Grove (Josh. 2:1; 3:1), about seven miles east of the Jordan River, almost directly across the river from Jericho. Joshua had been appointed as leader over the whole nation in Moses' place. In Joshua 1, the Lord reinforced Joshua's courage and resolve with a series of promises, and Joshua prepared the people to enter the land. The day this generation had hoped for all their lives was finally here.

God made promises to Joshua

Wisely, just as Moses had done years before, Joshua sent spies ahead to gather military and strategic information about what lay on the other side of the Jordan. This time, however, Joshua sent only two men, saying, "Go, view the land, especially Jericho" (2:1 NKJV).

Scripture says simply: "So they went, and came to the house of a harlot named Rahab, and lodged there" (2:1 NKJV). Thus Rahab is the very first person Scripture introduces us to in the Promised Land. By God's gracious providence, she would become one of the linchpins of Israel's military triumph. Her whole life, her career, and her future would be changed by her surprise encounter with two spies.

It is an unlikely confluence of forces for good: on the one hand, a lone pagan woman whose life up till now had been anything but heroic, and an entire nation of itinerant, lifelong refugees who had lived for the past forty years under the frown of God because of their parents' disobedience.

But the spies' collaboration with Rahab was the beginning of the downfall of Jericho. Jericho's defeat was the first dramatic conquest in one of history's greatest military campaigns ever.

AN UNEXPECTED ACT OF KINDNESS

Joshua 2:1–7 tells what happened:

> *Now Joshua the son of Nun sent out two men from Acacia Grove to spy secretly, saying, "Go, view the land, especially Jericho." So they went, and came to the house of a harlot named Rahab, and lodged there.*
>
> *And it was told the king of Jericho, saying, "Behold, men have come here tonight from the children of Israel to search out the country."*
>
> *So the king of Jericho sent to Rahab, saying, "Bring out the men who have come to you, who have entered your house, for they have come to search out all the country."*
>
> *Then the woman took the two men and hid them. So she said, "Yes, the men came to me, but I did not know where they were from.*
>
> *"And it happened as the gate was being shut, when it was dark, that the men went out. Where the men went I do not know; pursue them quickly, for you may overtake them."*
>
> *(But she had brought them up to the roof and hidden them with the stalks of flax, which she had laid in order on the roof.)*
>
> *Then the men pursued them by the road to the Jordan, to the fords. And as soon as those who pursued them had gone out, they shut the gate.* (NKJV)

Joshua deliberately kept the work of the spies secret. Apparently, even the Israelites did not know of their mission. The scouts were to report back to Joshua, not to the whole nation (vv. 23–24). Joshua wasn't asking them for feedback so that the people could discuss among themselves whether to go across the Jordan or hold back in fear. He wasn't about to make that mistake again. Israel had traveled down the dead-end road of popular opinion

✓
church

need for a decisive commander

already, and it cost them almost forty years' time. Joshua was taking the role of a decisive commander. He would assess the spies' report personally and decide (with the Lord's help, not a vote of the populace) how his armies would proceed.

Jericho was in a strategic location, at the openings of two vital pathways through the surrounding mountains, one leading southwest toward Jerusalem, the other leading northwest toward Ai and beyond, toward Bethel. Conquering Jericho would give Israel an important foothold into all the Promised Land. No wonder Jericho was so heavily fortified. The task of the spies was to assess those fortifications and report back to Joshua.

Most likely, the spies began their covert work shortly before dusk. The Jordan River lay seven miles to the west. A two-hour brisk walk would get them to the riverbank. There were fords nearby (v. 7), where the water ran approximately chest high at its deepest point. The men could either wade or easily swim across the Jordan. They would then have another seven-mile journey by foot to Jericho. (Even if they got wet crossing the river, this afforded more than enough time to be suitably dry upon arrival.) Then they would need to enter the walled city by some means and find lodging for the remainder of the night—all without arousing suspicion.

Jericho was a large town, and visitors came and went all the time. The spies managed to get into the city before the gates were closed for the night (v. 5). Scripture doesn't say how they got in. We assume they were able to find a way without much difficulty. Perhaps they simply mingled with other travelers at rush hour.

Once inside the city, the ideal place for lodging would be an inn or a house on the wall itself. From there they could assess the city's defenses. A good way to avoid arousing suspicion or attracting undue attention would be to find some seamy district where *everyone* would understand the need for discretion.

Their search led them to Rahab, a harlot, who was prosperous enough to have a house in a prime spot on the wall. Both she and her business were probably well-known in Jericho. Here was an ideal situation for the spies. She would have opened her door to them without any questions about who they were. In her business, the strictest confidentiality was essential. She would have welcomed them and invited them inside quickly, just as she did all her clients.

The Israelite spies did not seek her out to take advantage of her for immoral purposes, of course. Perhaps that very thing is what first won them her trust. They were obviously not there to use her or abuse her, unlike virtually all the other men she ever saw. They were serious and sober, but they did not seem to have frightened her in any way. Presumably, they treated her with patient dignity and respect while they made their careful reconnaissance. No doubt they explained who they were, which meant they would have almost certainly told her something about YHWH. Mostly, they went about their business, perhaps making measurements of the wall and recording details about the battlements and the landscape.

Rahab's house was perfect for their purposes. The position afforded a close-up look at the wall, which was the city's chief defense. But the location also made possible a quick escape if necessary. City walls are designed to keep out intruders, of course. But a person *on* the wall with a long enough rope can easily get out. By God's sovereign providence, everything they needed was in place. Also, by God's sovereign design, Rahab's heart was ready to believe in YHWH.

Somehow, it appears, the presence of the spies was known almost as soon as they entered Rahab's house. Of course, everyone in Jericho certainly already knew that the entire Israelite nation was camped across the river, within walking distance. All of Jericho had heard about Israel's miraculous escape from Pharaoh across the Red Sea and the drowning of the entire Egyptian army (v. 10). The story of Israel's subsequent wanderings in the wilderness was also well-known throughout the region. Rahab herself tells the spies that all the inhabitants of the land were fainthearted because of what they had heard about Israel and God's dealings with them. In Rahab's words, "As soon as we heard these things, our hearts melted; neither did there remain any more courage in anyone because of you" (v. 11 NKJV).

Still, aside from Rahab herself, the people of Jericho do not seem to have been *sufficiently* fearful of YHWH's power or Israel's military might. Perhaps the tales about forty years of aimless wandering had a tendency to counterbalance the Canaanites' fear over Israel's military might. Whatever the reason for their complacency, residents of Jericho were obviously too smug in the security of their walled fortress.

They were nonetheless on guard for intruders, and officials had probably given strict orders to report anything suspicious to the king. The "king" functioned like a city mayor, but he had military control. Therefore, he was the one to be notified if intruders were spotted.

Perhaps someone from whom the spies had asked directions turned them in. Or maybe sentries near Rahab's house spotted them and recognized them as Israelites from their clothing. In any case, their presence was quickly reported to Jericho's king. The information he received included exact details about where the spies had gone, so the king sent messengers to check out Rahab's house.

Here's where Rahab utterly surprises us. Remember, she made her living by selling herself for evil purposes. There was probably a handsome reward in it for her if she had turned in the spies. But she didn't. She hid them. She misdirected the officials and saved the lives of the two spies, even though this put her at considerable risk. Obviously, the king's representatives *knew* the spies had been in her home. When they were unable to find any evidence that the men had really left the city, they would probably be back to question Rahab again. She had put her own life in jeopardy by protecting these strangers. Her sudden expression of faith, therefore, is not only unexpected; it seems to run counter to every instinct that normally would motivate a woman like Rahab.

Rahab's actions in protecting the spies involved the telling of a lie. Was that justified? By commending her for her faith, is Scripture also condoning her methods? Good men have argued over that question, all the way back to the earliest rabbinical history. Let's face it. It is not an *easy* question. Scripture says, "Lying lips are an abomination to the LORD, but those who deal truthfully are His delight" (Prov. 12:22 NKJV). God Himself *cannot* lie (Titus 1:2; Num. 23:19; 1 Sam. 15:29), and therefore He cannot condone or sanction a lie. Some have tried to argue that because of the circumstances, this was not, technically, a "lie," but a military feint, a legitimate stratagem designed to trick or outwit the enemy in warfare. Others argue that even lying is acceptable if the motive is a greater good. Such a situational approach to ethics is fraught with very serious problems.

I see no need to try to justify Rahab's lie. Was it *necessary* for a greater good? Certainly not. Shadrach, Meshach, and Abednego might have escaped punishment by lying too. And they might have argued convincingly that it was for a "greater good." But there is no greater good than the truth, and the cause of truth can never be served by lying. Shadrach and friends told the truth—in fact they seized the opportunity to glorify God's name—and God was *still* able to save them from the furnace. He certainly could have saved Rahab and the spies without a lie.

Still, that isn't the point of Rahab's story. There's no need for clever rationalization to try to justify her lie. Scripture never commends *the lie*. Rahab isn't applauded for her *ethics*. Rahab is a positive example of *faith*.

At this moment, her faith was newborn, weak, and in need of nurture and growth. Her knowledge of YHWH was meager. (She makes it clear in Joshua 2:9–11 that she knew *something* about Him, having developed a keen interest in YHWH from the stories about Israel's escape from Egypt. But it's likely she had never met any true YHWH-worshipers before this night.) She most likely had no understanding of the value He put on truthfulness. Meanwhile, she was a product of a corrupt culture where ethics were virtually nonexistent. Lying was a way of life in her society—

and especially in her profession. The way she responded is just what we might expect from a brand-new believer under those circumstances.

The point is that Rahab's faith, undeveloped as it was, immediately bore the fruit of action. She "received the spies with peace" (Heb. 11:31 NKJV)—meaning that she not only hid them, but also implicitly embraced their cause. She thereby entrusted her whole future to their God. And the proof of her faith was not the lie she told, but the fact that "she received the messengers and sent them out another way" (James 2:25 NKJV)—when she might have handed them over for money instead. The *lie* is not what made her actions commendable. It was the fact that she turned down an easy reward, put herself in jeopardy, and thus staked everything on the God of Israel.

Nothing but faith could have made such a dramatic, instantaneous change in the character of such a woman. She had obviously developed a great curiosity about YHWH from the tales of His dealings with Israel. Now that she had met flesh-and-blood people who knew Him and worshiped Him, she was ready to throw her lot in with them.

AN AMAZING EXPRESSION OF FAITH

Rahab's quick thinking saved the spies. The narrative suggests that she quickly hid the men *after* the king's messengers knocked on her door and inquired about the spies. She heard the request, "*then* . . . took the two men and hid them," before giving an answer (Josh. 2:3–4 NKJV). The speed and ingenuity of her scheme to hide them suggests that she was experienced in this kind of thing. Apparently the stalks of flax, "which she had laid in order on the roof" (v. 6 NKJV), were there for precisely that purpose, in case a jealous wife came looking for a client. Rahab had a long rope handy too (v. 15 NKJV). No doubt she had arranged similar escapes, but for different reasons, in the past.

The hiding place certainly served a high and holy purpose this time.

Presumably, the king's messengers searched Rahab's house quickly and failed to find the spies before heading off in pursuit of the phony trail—which took them all the way to the fords of the Jordan.

After it was clear that the king's messengers were gone for the night, Rahab went back up to the roof to speak with the spies. She gave them an explicit testimony of the faith that motivated her. Here is the biblical account:

> *Now before they lay down, she came up to them on the roof, and said to the men: "I know that the LORD has given you the land, that the terror of you has fallen on us, and that all the inhabitants of the land are fainthearted because of you. For we have heard how the LORD dried up the water of the Red Sea for you when you came out of Egypt, and what you did to the two kings of the Amorites who were on the other side of the Jordan, Sihon and Og, whom you utterly destroyed. And as soon as we heard these things, our hearts melted; neither did there remain any more courage in anyone because of you,* for the LORD your God, He is God in heaven above and on earth beneath. *Now therefore, I beg you, swear to me by the LORD, since I have shown you kindness, that you also will show kindness to my father's house, and give me a true token, and spare my father, my mother, my brothers, my sisters, and all that they have, and deliver our lives from death."*
>
> *So the men answered her, "Our lives for yours, if none of you tell this business of ours. And it shall be, when the LORD has given us the land, that we will deal kindly and truly with you."*
>
> *Then she let them down by a rope through the window.* (Josh. 2:8–14 NKJV, emphasis added)

Notice that Rahab's faith was accompanied by *fear*. There is nothing wrong with that. Indeed, "The fear of the LORD is the beginning of wisdom" (Ps. 111:10 NKJV). In Rahab's case, fear is partly what motivated her faith. She had heard powerful evidence of the Lord's supremacy over Egypt. She understood that it was the Lord's might (not sheer military skill) that had triumphed over Sihon and Og, two fearsome Amorite kings (Josh. 2:10 NKJV). She probably understood something of YHWH's sovereign authority over Israel from the tales of their forty years in the wilderness. Hers was a healthy kind of fear. It had convinced her that YHWH was indeed the one true God. The psalmist wrote, "Men shall speak of the might of Your awesome acts, and I will declare Your greatness" (Ps. 145:6 NKJV). That is precisely the kind of testimony that had brought Rahab to faith.

The spies swore an oath to deal kindly with her when they conquered her city. But they gave her one condition. She was to hang a scarlet cord from the window where she let them down (Josh. 2:17–18). This would mark her house in the sight of all Israel, and anyone inside the house would be spared when the city was overthrown. The Hebrew word for "cord" in verse 18 is different from the word for "rope" in verse 15. This cord would have been a brightly colored band of woven threads, used for decorative purposes. The color would make it easily visible from beneath the wall. Both its appearance and its function were reminiscent of the crimson sign of the blood sprinkled on the doorposts at the first Passover. Many commentators believe the scarlet color is also a deliberate typological symbol for the blood of the true Paschal Lamb. Perhaps it is. It certainly stands as a fitting symbol of Christ's blood, which turns away the wrath of God.

From Rahab's perspective, however, the significance of the scarlet cord was nothing arcane or mystical. It was a simple, expedient emblem suited to mark her window discreetly so that her house would be easily distinguishable from all the rest of the houses in Jericho.

After making their solemn agreement to safeguard Rahab's household and sealing their pledge with an oath (vv. 17–20), the spies descended under cover of darkness via the rope into the valley outside Jericho's walls. Rahab had advised them to hide in the mountains for three days until the king gave up the search (v. 16), and they did so. Scripture says,

"The pursuers sought them all along the way, but did not find them" (v. 22 NKJV).

When the men finally returned to Joshua, their report contrasted sharply with the report the ten unfaithful spies had brought to Moses nearly forty years before. It was exactly what Joshua hoped to hear: "Truly the LORD has delivered all the land into our hands, for indeed all the inhabitants of the country are fainthearted because of us" (v. 24 NKJV).

AN ENDURING LEGACY

Israel's miraculous victory over Jericho is a familiar account to most people. It is a classic illustration of how spiritual triumph is always obtained: "'Not by might nor by power, but by My Spirit,' says the LORD of hosts" (Zech. 4:6 NKJV). God does not work exclusively by miracles. In fact, the times are relatively rare when He sets aside normal means in order to accomplish his purposes. Few of Israel's military battles were ever won solely by the miraculous intervention of God. The armies of Israel had to fight. But by the same token, *none* of their battles was ever won without the Lord's power.

In this case, God purposefully intervened in a way that made clear to everyone in Canaan that He was fighting for Israel. He demolished the massive walls of Jericho without any military means whatsoever. This was not a chance earthquake. To prove it, God had the Israelites march around the city with the ark of the covenant once each day for six consecutive days (Josh. 6). On the seventh day, they marched around the city seven times, blew a ram's horn, and shouted. Instantly, the wall of the city fell down flat (Josh. 6:20).

All except one part of the wall, that is. Rahab and her house were spared. "Joshua had said to the two men who had spied out the country, 'Go into the harlot's house, and from there bring out the woman and all that she has, as you swore to her.' And the young men who had been spies went in and brought out Rahab, her father, her mother, her brothers, and all that she had. So they brought out all her relatives and left them outside the camp of Israel" (vv. 22–23 NKJV). The writer of Joshua (probably Joshua himself) added, "So she dwells in Israel to this day" (v. 25 NKJV).

Rahab is a beautiful example of the transforming power of faith. Although she had few spiritual advantages and little knowledge of the truth, her heart was drawn to YHWH. She risked her life, turned her back on a way of life that did not honor God, and walked away from everything but her closest family members (whom she brought into the community of God's people along with her). From that day on, she lived a completely different kind of life, as a true hero of faith. She has a place of honor in Hebrews 11 alongside some notable names in that "great cloud of witnesses" who testify to the saving power of faith.

After the account of Jericho's destruction in Joshua 6, Rahab is never again mentioned by name in the Old Testament. Of course, when Joshua noted that Rahab was still living in Israel, this was probably many years after the fall of Jericho. Apparently, she lived out her life in quiet dignity and grace amid the people of God. She was wholly changed from the kind of woman she once had been. She was, and is still, a living symbol of the transforming effect of saving faith. That is the primary message of her life.

In fact, when we *do* meet Rahab again on the pages of Scripture, it is in the New Testament. Her name is mentioned there three times. Two of those honor her for her remarkable faith (Heb. 11:31; James 2:25). She is held up as an example of faith for both men and women. James, in particular, cites her case to show that faith produces action. Indeed, Rahab's faith did not lie dormant long. Remember, it was only after she hid the spies that she verbalized to them her belief that YHWH was the one true God. Her faith was seen in the fruit of her works before she even had an opportunity to verbalize it on her tongue. James says genuine faith is always active and fruitful like that. "Faith without works is dead" (James 2:26 NKJV). Rahab's faith was anything but dead.

The most amazing occurrence of Rahab's name, though, in the New Testament is the very first time it appears there, on the very first page, in the very first paragraph of the first gospel. Matthew began his account of Christ's life with a lengthy genealogy tracing the entire lineage of Jesus from the time of Abraham. Matthew's goal, of course, was to prove by Jesus' pedigree that He qualified to be the promised Seed of Abraham, and that He is also rightful heir to the Davidic throne. There, in the list of Jesus' ancestors, we unexpectedly find Rahab's name: "Salmon begot Boaz by Rahab, Boaz begot Obed by Ruth, Obed begot Jesse" (Matt. 1:5 NKJV).

It is highly unusual for women to be named in Hebrew genealogies at all. (Notice that the record of Adam's offspring in Genesis 5 omits any reference to his daughters.) Yet Matthew mentions five women, and all of them are notable: Tamar (1:3), Rahab (v. 5), Ruth (v. 5), Bathsheba (v. 6), and Mary (v. 16). At least three of them were Gentiles. Three of them were disgraced because of their own sin. In fact, all of them, for various reasons, knew what it was to be an outcast—to have some infamy or stigma attached to their reputations:

- Tamar was a Canaanite woman whose husband had died, leaving her childless. She posed as a prostitute and seduced her own father-in-law, Judah, in order to bear a child. Interestingly enough, a scarlet thread also plays a role in Tamar's tragic life story (Gen. 38:13–30).

- Rahab we already know about, including the shame of her sordid background.

- Ruth (whom we will soon meet) was from the Moabite nation, a people generally despised in Israel (Ruth 1:3).

- Bathsheba (whom Matthew doesn't name but refers to simply as "the wife of Uriah") committed adultery with King David (2 Sam. 11).

- Mary, of course, bore the disgrace of an out-of-wedlock pregnancy.

Collectively, they illustrate how God is able to work all things together for good. From a human perspective, the whole genealogy is checkered with outcasts and examples of failure. The women, in particular, underscore how scandal colored so much of the messianic line. It was filled with foreigners, outcasts, and those who were pariahs for various reasons. Still, they nevertheless all found a place in the plan of God to bring His Son into the world.

The scandal motif in Christ's lineage was no accident. In His incarnation, Christ willingly "made Himself of no reputation, taking the form of a bondservant" (Phil. 2:7 NKJV). He *became* an outcast and a public disgrace, being made a curse on our behalf (Gal. 3:13). He remains even now "a stone of stumbling and a rock of offense" (1 Peter 2:8 NKJV). The gospel message, too, is a public scandal—mere foolishness and shame as far as those who perish are concerned. But to those who are saved, it is the power of God (1 Cor. 1:18).

Then again, "Those who are well have no need of a physician, but those who are sick. [Christ] did not come to call the righteous, but sinners, to repentance" (Mark 2:17 NKJV). Rahab was the very embodiment of that truth. This is why the New Testament repeatedly brings her up as a real-life example of the fruit of saving faith. She is a living reminder that even the worst of sinners can be redeemed by divine grace through faith. "For by grace you have been saved through faith, and that *not of yourselves;* it is the gift of God, not of works, lest anyone should boast. For we are *His* workmanship" (Eph. 2:8–10 NKJV, emphasis added).

Rahab was redeemed not because of any meritorious works she did. She did not earn God's favor by any good deeds. Remember, even what she *did* do right—harboring the spies—was morally tainted because of the way she handled it. She lied. But she is not given to us as an example of the power of human works. She is not a lesson in how to better ourselves through self-improvement. She is a reminder that God by *His* grace can redeem even the most horrible life.

Some of the scholastic rabbis just prior to Jesus' time became embarrassed by the fact that a woman with Rahab's background was spared in the destruction of Jericho and brought into Israel as a proselyte. They proposed a different understanding of the Hebrew word for *harlot* in Joshua 2:1 (also 6:17, 25). The Hebrew term is similar to a word meaning "to feed," they claimed. Perhaps Rahab was really just an innkeeper or a hostess, they countered.

The problem is, the actual Hebrew word really can mean only one thing: "harlot." That was the uncontested understanding of this text for centuries. In fact, there is no ambiguity whatsoever in the Septuagint (an ancient Greek translation of the Old Testament dating to the second century BC) or in the Greek texts of Hebrews 11:31 and James 2:25. The Greek word used to describe Rahab is *porne,* meaning "harlot." (Notice that the term comes from the same root as the English term *pornography* and has similar negative moral overtones.)

The idea of sanitizing Rahab's background was revived by some churchmen with overly delicate sensibilities in the Victorian era. C. H. Spurgeon, the best-known Baptist preacher in late nineteenth-century London, replied, "This woman was no mere hostess, but a real harlot . . . I am persuaded that nothing but a spirit of distaste for free grace would ever have led any commentator to deny her sin."

He was exactly right, of course. Remove the stigma of sin, and you remove the need for grace. Rahab is extraordinary precisely because she received extraordinary grace. There's no need to reinvent her past to try to make her seem less of a sinner. The disturbing fact about what she once *was* simply magnifies the glory of divine grace, which is what made her the extraordinary woman she *became.* That, after all, is the whole lesson of her life.

4

RUTH: LOYALTY AND LOVE

Your people shall be my people, and your God, my God.

Ruth 1:16 NKJV

The Old Testament book of Ruth is a flawless love story in a compact format. It's not an epic tale, but a short story. (The entire account is given in only eighty-five verses.) Still, it runs the full range of human emotions, from the most gut-wrenching kind of grief to the very height of glad-hearted triumph.

Ruth's life was the true, historical experience of one genuinely extraordinary woman. It was also a perfect depiction of the story of redemption, told with living, breathing symbols. Ruth herself furnished a fitting picture of every sinner. She was a widow and a foreigner who went to live in a strange land. Tragic circumstances reduced her to abject poverty. She was not only an outcast and an exile, but also bereft of any resources—reduced to a state of utter destitution from which she could never hope to redeem herself by *any* means. In her extremity, she sought the grace of her mother-in-law's closest kinsman. The story of how her whole life was changed is one of the most deeply touching narratives in the whole of Scripture.

RUIN

Ruth's story began near the end of the era of the Judges in the Old Testament. It was about a century before the time of David, in an age that was often characterized by anarchy, confusion, and unfaithfulness to the law of God. There was also a severe famine in Israel in those days.

We are introduced to the family of Elimelech in Ruth 1:1–2. Elimelech had a wife, Naomi, and two sons, named Mahlon and Chilion. Their hometown was Bethlehem, famous as the burial place of Rachel, Jacob's wife (Gen. 35:19). Bethlehem in future generations would gain more lasting fame as the hometown of David, and then, of course, as the birthplace of Christ. The story of Elimelech's family became a key link in the chain tying the messianic line to Bethlehem.

The famine in Israel forced Elimelech and family to seek refuge in Moab, just as a similar famine had once driven Abraham into Egypt. These must have been desperate times, because Moab itself was a mostly desolate region, a high tableland bounded on the west by the Dead Sea and on the east by arid desert wasteland. Its boundaries on the north and south were two deep river gorges (the Arnon and the Zered, respectively), and these were virtually dry most of the year. Moab was fertile but dry, and therefore the land was largely destitute of trees, good mostly for grazing flocks and herds.

The Moabites were descendants of Lot's eldest daughter through her incestuous relationship with her own father. The child born of that illicit union was named Moab. He was, of course, a second cousin of Jacob. (Remember that Lot was Abraham's nephew.) But even though their ancestries had that close relationship, the Moabites and the Israelites generally despised one another.

During the time of Israel's wilderness wanderings, Moabite women deliberately seduced Israelite men, then enticed them to participate in sacrifices to idolatrous gods (Num. 25). Moab was the same nation whose king, Balak, engaged the hireling prophet, Balaam, to prophesy against Israel. So throughout the Old Testament, relations between Israel and Moab ranged from uneasy tension to outright hostility.

The Moabites worshiped a god whom they called Chemosh. (He was their chief deity, but Numbers 25:2 suggests that they worshiped many others also.) Scripture calls Chemosh "the abomination of Moab" (1 Kings 11:7; 2 Kings 23:13 NKJV). Worship of this idol was grotesque, at times even involving human sacrifices (2 Kings 3:26–27). As the events of Numbers 25 suggest, Moabite worship was also filled with erotic imagery and lewd conduct. Moabite paganism typified everything abominable about idolatry. The Moabite culture practically epitomized everything faithful Israelites were supposed to shun.

We are therefore meant to be somewhat shocked and appalled by the fact that Elimelech and family sought refuge in Moab. Elimelech was a landowner in Bethlehem, and prominent enough to be called "our brother" by the city elders there (Ruth 4:2–3 NKJV). His name means, "My God is king." That, together with Naomi's faith and character, suggests that he and his family were devout Jews, not careless worldlings. The fact that Elimelech would take his family to Moab is a measure of the famine's frightening severity. The land of Israel was evidently both spiritually and physically parched, and times were desperate.

Tragedy quickly mounted for this family. First, Elimelech died in Moab, leaving Naomi a widow with the responsibility of two sons. Fortunately for her, Mahlon and Chilion were approaching adulthood, and they soon married. Unfortunately, the wives they took were Moabites (Ruth 1:3–4). No devout Israelite would have regarded such a marriage as auspicious. Israelite men were expressly forbidden to marry Canaanite women, lest the men be turned away to other gods (Deut. 7:1–3). Common sense suggests that for similar reasons, marriage to a Moabite wasn't deemed appropriate, either. Nevertheless, Naomi and her sons must have felt trapped by their desperate circumstances, so Naomi seems to have graciously accepted these daughters-in-law. One was named Orpah (meaning "stubborn") and the other, Ruth ("friendship"). Ruth

Ruth
married
Mahlon

RUTH

Orpah
married
Chilion

married Mahlon (Ruth 4:10), who was apparently the elder of the two sons. Orpah, then, would have been the wife of Chilion. Ruth 1:4 says Naomi and her sons dwelt in Moab ten years. (That is probably the total time they spent in Moab rather than the amount of time that passed after the young men married, because neither of the young couples seem to have had children. That would have been very unusual after ten years of marriage, even in a time of famine.)

Meanwhile, circumstances did not appear to be improving for Naomi. In fact, matters took a turn for the worse. Both Mahlon and Chilion died, leaving the three women to fend for themselves. In that culture, this was a nearly impossible situation. Three widows, with no children and no responsible relatives, in a time of famine, could not hope to survive for long, even if they pooled their meager resources. We're not told what caused any of the husbands to die, but the fact that all three perished is a measure of how hard life was in the adversity of those days. Mahlon and Chilion seem to have died in quick succession, suggesting they perhaps fell victim to a disease, very likely related to the famine.

Naomi, Ruth, and Orpah had been brought to the brink of ruin. So when word reached Naomi that the drought was broken in Israel, she quickly made up her mind to return. She was now childless, widowed, impoverished, and aging (Ruth 1:12), destitute of all land and possessions, and without any relatives close enough to count on them to care for her. Still, she longed for her homeland and her own people, and she decided to go back to Bethlehem.

Both daughters-in-law began the difficult journey with Naomi, but as Naomi considered their circumstances (especially the hardships these two young women might face if they staked their futures to hers), she decided to release them back to their own families. It seemed to Naomi as if the hand of the Lord was against her (v. 13). She no doubt struggled with bitter regret over having come to Moab in the first place. Now she would be leaving her husband and both of her sons buried in that God-forsaken place. She seems to have been overcome with remorse and perhaps a feeling that she had somehow incurred the Lord's displeasure by going to Moab. Why should her daughters-in-law suffer because God's hand of discipline was against her? So she tried to persuade the young women to turn back.

The biblical description of the scene—especially the bitter anguish shared by all three women—is heart-rending:

Then she arose with her daughters-in-law that she might return from the country of Moab, for she had heard in the country of Moab that the LORD had visited His people by giving them bread. Therefore she went out from the place where she was, and her two daughters-in-law with her; and they went on the way to return to the land of Judah. And Naomi said to her two daughters-in-law, "Go, return each to her mother's house. The LORD deal kindly with you, as you have dealt with the dead and with me. The LORD grant that you may find rest, each in the house of her husband." Then she kissed them, and they lifted up their voices and wept.

And they said to her, "Surely we will return with you to your people."

But Naomi said, "Turn back, my daughters; why will you go with me? Are there still sons in my womb, that they may be your husbands? Turn back, my daughters, go; for I am too old to have a husband. If I should say I have hope, if I should have a husband tonight and should also bear sons, would you wait for them till they were grown? Would you restrain yourselves from having husbands? No, my daughters; for it grieves me very much for your sakes that the hand of the LORD has gone out against me!"

Then they lifted up their voices and wept again; and Orpah kissed her mother-in-law, but Ruth clung to her. (Ruth 1:6–14 NKJV)

RESOLVE

Ruth was determined to stay with Naomi, regardless of the personal cost. The still-young Moabite girl probably felt that she quite literally had nothing left to lose anyway. In keeping with the meaning of her name, Ruth seems to have developed a close bond of friendship and attachment to her mother-in-law.

Naomi still tried to dissuade Ruth from going any farther with her. "She said, 'Look, your sister-in-law has gone back to her people and to her gods; return after your sister-in-law'" (Ruth 1:15 NKJV). Naomi no doubt felt it was not in Ruth's best interests to be shackled to an aged widow. On the other hand, she certainly could not have truly believed that it would be a good thing for Ruth to go back to her people *and to her gods.*" In all likelihood, Naomi was testing Ruth, hoping to coax from her an explicit verbal profession of faith in YHWH. It would be wrong to take Ruth to Israel and place a widow without financial support in that society if she had no genuine commitment to Israel's God.

Ruth's reply is a beautiful piece of poetry in Hebrew style:

> *Entreat me not to leave you,*
> *Or to turn back from following after you;*
> *For wherever you go, I will go;*
> *And wherever you lodge, I will lodge;*
> *Your people shall be my people,*
> *And your God, my God.*
> *Where you die, I will die,*
> *And there will I be buried.*
> *The LORD do so to me, and more also,*
> *If anything but death parts you and me.* (Ruth 1:16–17 NKJV)

Thus Ruth expressed her firm resolve to stay with Naomi. Her affection for her mother-in-law was sincere. She still desired to remain part of that family. Above all, her devotion to the God of Israel was real. This was an amazingly mature and meaningful testimony of personal faith, especially in light of the fact that it came from the lips of a young woman raised in a pagan culture. The witness of Naomi and her family must have made a powerful impression on Ruth.

When Naomi saw the firm resolve of Ruth, Scripture says, "she stopped speaking to her" (v. 18 NKJV)—meaning, of course, that she gave up trying to dissuade Ruth from coming with her to Bethlehem. Their souls and their destinies were bound together by their friendship and their common faith.

After ten years or more in Moab, Naomi returned to people who remembered her and knew her name. Naomi's return caused no small stir. Scripture says, "All the city was excited because of them; and the women said, 'Is this Naomi?'" (v. 19 NKJV). *Naomi* means "pleasant," and in an earlier time it must have been a perfect description of Naomi. The fact that so many women remembered her and were so glad to see her suggests that she had once been a gregarious soul, beloved by all who knew her. But now her life was so colored with sadness that she told the other women, "Do not call me Naomi; call me Mara [meaning 'bitter'], for the Almighty has dealt very bitterly with me. I went out full, and the LORD has brought me home again empty. Why do you call me Naomi, since the LORD has testified against me, and the Almighty has afflicted me?" (vv. 20–21 NKJV).

This was not a complaint as much as a heartfelt lament. She knew, as Job did, that it is the Lord who gives and takes away. She understood the principle of God's sovereignty. In calling herself "Mara," she was not suggesting that she had become a bitter person; but (as her words reveal) that Providence had handed her a bitter cup to drink. She saw the hand of God in her sufferings, but far from complaining, I think she was simply acknowledging her faith in the sovereignty of God, even in the midst of a life of bitter grief. Everything Scripture tells us about Naomi indicates that she remained steadfast in the faith throughout her trials. She was not unlike Job—she was a woman of great faith who withstood almost unimaginable testing without ever once wavering in her love for YHWH and her commitment to His will. So hers is actually an impressive expression of faith, without an ounce of resentment in it.

Elimelech had a wealthy relative named Boaz, who had prospered despite the years of famine. He was a landowner of vast holdings and considerable influence. Scripture says he was "a relative of Naomi's husband" (Ruth 2:1 NKJV), but does not spell out the relationship. He might have been Elimelech's brother, but that seems unlikely, since he wasn't, technically, Naomi's next of kin (Ruth 3:12). He was more likely a cousin or a nephew of Elimelech.

Boaz was also a direct descendant of Rahab. Matthew 1:5 says, "Salmon begot Boaz by Rahab" (NKJV), and that agrees with Ruth 4:21, but the number of years spanning the time between the fall of Jericho and the start of the Davidic dynasty suggest that there must be more generations between Salmon and David than either Matthew 1 or Ruth 4 explicitly name. Hebrew genealogy often used a kind of shorthand, skipping generations between well-known ancestors. Matthew seems to do this deliberately to achieve a kind of numerical symmetry in the genealogical listing (Matt. 1:17)—probably as an aid to memorization. So rather than being the immediate son of Rahab, Boaz may very well have been a great-grandson. He was nonetheless in Rahab's direct line. He undoubtedly knew her story well and gloried in his heritage. His connection with Rahab would certainly have inclined his heart to be sympathetic to the plight of a foreign woman like Ruth who had embraced YHWH with a faith reminiscent of Rahab's.

REDEMPTION

In agreeing to return to Bethlehem with Naomi, Ruth was agreeing to help support the aging woman. The biblical data suggest that Ruth was still quite young and physically strong. So she went to work in the fields, gleaning what the harvesters left behind in order to provide enough grain to eke out an existence.

Biblical law established this as a means by which even the most destitute in Israel could always earn a living. Leviticus 19:9–10; 23:22, and Deuteronomy 24:19–21 all required that when a field was harvested, whatever fell from the sheaves should be deliberately left behind. When fruit was picked from trees and vines, some of it was to be left unplucked. The remains of the harvest were then free to be gleaned by anyone willing to do the work.

Ruth's options were limited to that, and that alone. She had no relatives other than her mother-in-law. Naomi's own next of kin weren't even close enough to be legally obliged to support her. With no visible means of support, Ruth saw the necessity of working the barley fields, so she sought and obtained Naomi's permission (Ruth 2:2).

As it happened, she gleaned in one of Boaz's fields, and he saw her. The language of the text suggests that this was purely by happenstance—"she happened to come to the part of the field belonging to Boaz" (v. 3 NKJV)—but we know from the clear teaching of Scripture that God Himself providentially orchestrated these events (Prov. 16:33). Nothing happens by "chance," but God is always behind the scenes, working all things together for the good of His people (Rom. 8:28). There is no such thing as "luck" or "fate" for believers.

Boaz visited his fields that very day, to see the progress of the harvest. When he noticed Ruth, he took an immediate interest. She was obviously young, able, and diligent. Boaz sought out the foreman of his crew and inquired about Ruth.

The chief servant replied, "It is the young Moabite woman who came back with Naomi from the country of Moab. And she said, 'Please let me glean and gather after the reapers among the sheaves.' So she came and has continued from morning until now, though she rested a little in the house" (Ruth 2:6–7 NKJV).

Boaz immediately realized, of course, that this woman was his relative by marriage, so he began to show her special favor. He encouraged her to glean only in his fields and to stay close by his harvesters. He gave her permission to drink from the water he supplied his servants, and he instructed his young men not to touch her.

Ruth, moved by his gentle kindness and generosity, knew very well that such extreme liberality was highly unusual, especially toward an impoverished woman from a foreign land. "She fell on her face, bowed down to the ground, and said to him, 'Why have I found favor in your eyes, that you should take notice of me, since I am a foreigner?'" (v. 10 NKJV).

Boaz explained that he had heard of her extraordinary faithfulness to Naomi and the great sacrifices she had made to come to a foreign land. Then he gave her an unusual blessing that reveals what a godly man he was: "The LORD repay your work, and a full reward be given you by the LORD God of Israel, under whose wings you have come for refuge" (v. 12 NKJV).

Her reply was equally gracious, and beautiful for its humility: "Let me find favor in your sight, my lord; for you have comforted me, and have spoken kindly to your maidservant, though I am not like one of your maidservants" (v. 13 NKJV).

In that first meeting, Boaz immediately seemed smitten with Ruth. He invited her to eat with his workers at mealtime and personally saw that she had enough to be satisfied (vv. 14–16). He instructed his workers to permit her to glean among his sheaves, and he even encouraged them to let grain fall purposely from the bundles for her sake. Thus he lightened the load of her labor and increased the reward of it.

Ruth nonetheless continued to work hard all day. "She gleaned in the field until evening, and beat out what she had gleaned, and it was about an ephah of barley" (v. 17 NKJV). That was a full half bushel, approximately enough to sustain Ruth and Naomi for five days or more. This was about four times as much as a gleaner could hope to gather on a typical good day. Ruth took the grain, as well as some leftover food from lunch, and gave it to Naomi.

Naomi was clearly surprised and pleased at Ruth's amazing prosperity.

She seemed to have instinctively understood that Ruth could not possibly have done so well without someone's help. So she asked where Ruth had gleaned and pronounced a special blessing on "the one who took notice of you" (v. 19 NKJV).

When Ruth told her the man who had been her benefactor was named Boaz, Naomi instantly saw the hand of God in the blessing. "Naomi said to her daughter-in-law, 'Blessed be he of the LORD, who has not forsaken His kindness to the living and the dead!' And Naomi said to her, 'This man is a relation of ours, one of our close relatives'" (v. 20 NKJV).

The Hebrew word translated "one of our close relatives" is *goel.* It is a technical term that means much more than "kinsman." The *goel* was a relative who came to the rescue. The word *goel* includes the idea of redemption, or deliverance. In fact, in order to express the idea more perfectly in English, Old Testament scholars sometimes speak of the *goel* as a "kinsman-redeemer." In Scripture, the word is sometimes translated as "redeemer" (Job 19:25 NKJV) and sometimes as "avenger" (Num. 35:12 NKJV).

A *goel* was usually a prominent male in one's extended family. He was the official guardian of the family's honor. If the occasion arose, he would be the one to avenge the blood of a murdered relative (Josh. 20:2–9). He could buy back family lands sold in times of hardship (Lev. 25:23–28). He could pay the redemption-price for family members sold into slavery (Lev. 25:47–49). Or (if he were a single man or widower and thus eligible to marry) he could revive the family lineage when someone died without an heir by marrying the widow and fathering offspring who would inherit the name and the property of the one who had died. This was known as the law of levirate marriage, and Deuteronomy 25:5–10 presented it as a *duty* in cases where one brother (obviously unmarried and presumably younger) was living in the household of a married brother who died. If the surviving brother refused to fulfill the duty of the *goel* by marrying his brother's widow, he was treated with contempt by all of society.

The Old Testament places a great deal of emphasis on the role of the *goel.* There was a significant redemptive aspect to this person's function. Every kinsman-redeemer was, in effect, a living illustration of the position and work of Christ with respect to His people: He is our true Kinsman-Redeemer, who becomes our human Brother, buys us back from our bondage to evil, redeems our lives from death, and ultimately returns to us everything we lost because of our sin.

Boaz would become Ruth's *goel.* He would redeem her life from poverty and widowhood. He would be her deliverer—and Naomi grasped the potential of this glad turn of events the very moment she learned it was Boaz who had taken an interest in Ruth. He was not only a kinsman; he had the means to be a redeemer too. Naomi strongly encouraged Ruth to follow Boaz's instructions and stay exclusively in his fields. Ruth did this until the end of the harvest season (Ruth 2:21–23).

Naomi saw it as her duty as mother-in-law to seek long-term security for this faithful Moabite girl who had so graciously proven her loyalty, generosity, diligence, and strength of character throughout the hot and difficult harvest season. In a culture where arranged marriages were the norm, this meant doing what she could to orchestrate a marriage between Ruth and Boaz.

Because she was a woman, protocol forbade Naomi from approaching Boaz to arrange a marriage for Ruth. In fact, there was no suggestion that Naomi had spoken to Boaz at all about anything since her return from Moab. Yet from the very beginning, Naomi clearly had an intuition about Boaz's interest in Ruth. Having watched and waited through the long harvest season, Naomi apparently decided Boaz needed some subtle help to get the ball rolling. The way things finally played out suggests that Naomi's instincts were right on target.

If Boaz had ever been married, Scripture does not mention it. According to Jewish tradition, he was a lifelong bachelor. He may have had some physical imperfection or personality quirk that stood in the way of a suitable marriage arrangement. At the very least, he desperately needed prodding. Although he obviously took a keen interest in Ruth from the moment he first saw her, it does not seem to have entered his mind to pursue the *goel's* role on her behalf. By his own testimony (Ruth 3:10), he was surprised that Ruth didn't deem him unsuitable for marriage.

Naomi had sized up the situation correctly though, and she instructed Ruth on what to do. Naomi's scheme was bold and utterly unconventional. Of course, Ruth, as a foreigner, could always plead ignorance of Jewish custom, but if Naomi's plan had been known in advance by people in the community, the propriety police certainly would have been up in arms. Of course, the scheme did not involve any *real* unrighteousness or indecency. Naomi certainly would not have asked Ruth to compromise her virtue or relinquish godly modesty.

Still, what Naomi advised Ruth to do was shockingly forward. (Even to enlightened twenty-first-century minds, it seems surprisingly plucky.) Naomi's plan, in essence, was for Ruth to propose marriage to Boaz! She told Ruth, "Wash yourself and anoint yourself, put on your best garment and go down to the threshing floor; but do not make yourself known to the man until he has finished eating and drinking. Then it shall be, when he lies down, that you shall notice the place where he lies; and you shall go in, uncover his feet, and lie down; and he will tell you what you should do" (Ruth 3:3–4 NKJV). By the custom of the time, this would indicate Ruth's willingness to marry Boaz.

It was the end of the harvest. The threshing floor was a site, most likely out of doors, where grain was winnowed. This involved tossing grain into the air in a breeze so that the light husks of chaff would be blown away. Boaz would work late, sleep outdoors at the threshing floor all night, then arise early and go back to threshing. Thus he both extended his work hours and guarded his grain through the night. He worked well into the night, had a short meal, and laid down next to the grain pile to sleep. Scripture says "his heart was cheerful" (Ruth 3:7 NKJV).

The harvest had been abundant. After years of famine, Boaz was exhilarated at his prosperity.

In accordance with Naomi's instructions, Ruth "came softly, uncovered his feet, and lay down" (v. 7 NKJV). Boaz was so fatigued that he did not notice her until he awakened at midnight and was startled to find a woman lying at his feet.

He said, "Who are you?"

She answered, "I am Ruth, your maidservant. Take your maidservant under your wing, for you are a *[goel]*" (v. 9 NKJV). Ruth was borrowing language ("under your wing") from the blessing Boaz had given her (2:12). This was, in effect, a marriage proposal.

This came as an overwhelming and unexpected blessing to Boaz. According to Ruth 3:10–13:

> *Then he said, "Blessed are you of the LORD, my daughter! For you have shown more kindness at the end than at the beginning, in that you did not go after young men, whether poor or rich. And now, my daughter, do not fear. I will do for you all that you request, for all the people of my town know that you are a virtuous woman. Now it is true that I am a close relative; however, there is relative closer than I. Stay this night, and in the morning it shall be that if he will perform the duty of a close relative for you—good; let him do it. But if he does not want to perform the duty for you, then I will perform the duty for you, as the LORD lives! Lie down until morning."* (NKJV)

Scripture doesn't identify the man who was Naomi's actual next of kin. (He would almost certainly have been either an older brother or cousin of Boaz.) Boaz knew immediately who it was, and he knew that custom required him to defer to this other relative. He explained the situation to Ruth, swore to her his own willingness to be her *goel* if it were possible, and urged her to remain at his feet through the night.

Nothing immoral occurred, of course, and Scripture is clear about that. But Boaz, being protective of Ruth's virtue, awoke her and sent her home just before dawn. He gave her a generous portion of grain as a gift for Naomi, saying, "Do not go empty-handed to your mother-in-law" (v. 17 NKJV).

Naomi, of course, was anxiously awaiting word of what had happened. Ruth told her the whole story, and Naomi, whose feminine intuition was impeccable, said, "Sit still, my daughter, until you know how the matter will turn out; for the man will not rest until he has concluded the matter this day" (v. 18 NKJV).

She was exactly right. Boaz went immediately to the city gate and found Naomi's true next of kin. The two of them sat down in the presence of ten city elders and negotiated for the right to be Ruth's *goel.*

That role involved, first of all, the buy-back of Elimelech's property. In Israel, land portions were part of each family's lasting legacy from generation to generation. Plots of family land could not be permanently sold (Lev. 25:23). Real estate that was "sold" to pay debts remained in the possession of the buyer only until the year of Jubilee, at which time it reverted to the original owner's family. This arrangement helped keep Israel's wealth evenly distributed, and it meant that land-sale deals were actually more like long-term leases. Land sold for debt relief could also be redeemed at any time by the seller or his *goel.* As long as Elimelech had no heirs, the property he and Naomi had sold to pay their debts would automatically become the permanent possession of anyone who acted as Naomi's *goel* by redeeming her property. This made the prospect extremely appealing.

Boaz said, "If you will redeem it, redeem it; but if you will not redeem it, then tell me, that I may know; for there is no one but you to redeem it, and I am next after you."

"I will redeem it," the other relative replied (Ruth 4:4 NKJV).

But then Boaz explained that there was a catch. While Elimelech had no surviving heir, the man who would have been his rightful heir (Mahlon) had left a widow. Therefore, Boaz explained, "On the day you buy the field from the hand of Naomi, you must also buy it from Ruth the Moabitess, the wife of the dead, to perpetuate the name of the dead through his inheritance" (v. 5 NKJV).

This changed things a bit. Because if Ruth *did* remarry someone under the principle of levirate marriage, and she produced any heir in Mahlon's name, rights to Elimelech's land would automatically pass to Ruth's offspring. The only way to eliminate that risk would be to marry Ruth. The unnamed close relative was either unable or unwilling to marry Ruth. And he didn't want to take an expensive risk that might jeopardize his own children's inheritance. So he told Boaz, "I cannot redeem it for myself, lest I ruin my own inheritance. You redeem my right of redemption for yourself, for I cannot redeem it" (v. 6 NKJV).

A formal contract was then publicly sealed in the customary fashion: the relative removed his sandal and gave it to Boaz (v. 8), in effect granting Boaz the right to stand in his stead as *goel* for Ruth and Naomi.

And Boaz said to the elders and all the people, "You are witnesses this day that I have bought all that was Elimelech's, and all that was Chilion's and Mahlon's, from the hand of Naomi. Moreover, Ruth the Moabitess, the widow of Mahlon, I have acquired as my wife, to perpetuate the name of the dead through his inheritance, that the name of the dead may not be cut off from among his brethren and from his position at the gate. You are witnesses this day" (vv. 9–10 NKJV).

Everyone loves a good love story, and the people of Bethlehem were no exception. As word got out about the unusual transaction taking place in the city gate, the inhabitants of the city began to congregate. They pronounced a blessing on Boaz and his bride-to-be. "We are witnesses," they told Boaz. "The LORD make the woman who is coming to your house like Rachel and Leah, the two who built the house of Israel; and may you prosper in Ephrathah and be famous in Bethlehem. May your house be like the house of Perez, whom Tamar bore to Judah, because of the offspring which the LORD will give you from this young woman" (vv. 11:1–12 NKJV).

The blessing proved to be prophetic. Boaz and Ruth were married, and the Lord soon blessed them with a son. At the birth of this child, the women of Bethlehem gave a blessing to Naomi as well: "Blessed be the LORD, who has not left you this day without a close relative; and may his name be famous in Israel! And may he be to you a restorer of life and a nourisher of your old age; for your daughter-in-law, who loves you, who is better to you than seven sons, has borne him" (vv. 14–15 NKJV).

All of that came true as well. As verse 17 explains, "The neighbor women gave him a name, saying, 'There is a son born to Naomi.' And they called his name Obed. He is the father of Jesse, the father of David" (NKJV). In other words, Ruth was David's great-grandmother.

That is how Ruth, a seemingly ill-fated Moabite woman whose loyalty and faith had led her away from her own people and carried her as a stranger into the land of Israel, became a mother in the royal line that would eventually produce that nation's first great king. Her best-known offspring would be Abraham's Seed and Eve's hoped-for Deliverer.

Ruth is a fitting symbol of every believer, and even of the church itself—redeemed, brought into a position of great favor, endowed with riches and privilege, exalted to be the Redeemer's own bride, and loved by Him with the profoundest affection. That is why the extraordinary story of her redemption ought to make every true believer's heart resonate with profound gladness and thanksgiving for the One who, likewise, has redeemed us from our sin.

5

Hannah: A Portrait of Feminine Grace

Hannah prayed and said: "My heart rejoices in the LORD; My horn is exalted in the LORD. I smile at my enemies, Because I rejoice in Your salvation."

1 Samuel 2:1 NKJV

Hannah's name means "grace." It's a fitting designation for a woman whose life was crowned with grace and who became a living emblem of the grace of motherhood. A study of her life reveals the classic profile of a godly mother.

Yet Hannah almost despaired of ever *becoming* a mother. Her experience strongly echoes Sarah's. Like Sarah, she was childless and distraught over it. Both women's marriages were plagued with stress because of their husbands' bigamy. Both of them ultimately received the blessing they sought from God, and in both cases, the answers to their prayers turned out to be exceedingly and abundantly more significant than they had ever dared to ask or think. Hannah's son, Samuel, was the last of the judges. He was also a priest—the one who formally inaugurated the true royal line of Israel by anointing David as king. Samuel became a towering figure in Israel's history. Thus Hannah's life often mirrored that of the original matriarch, Sarah. Most of all, she mirrored Sarah's amazing faith and perseverance.

In a similar way, Hannah also foreshadowed Mary, the mother of Jesus. Hannah's prayer of dedication in 1 Samuel 2:1–10 was the model for Mary's Magnificat in Luke 1:46–55. Both Hannah and Mary formally dedicated their firstborn sons to the Lord (1 Sam. 1:24–28; Luke 2:22–24). Surrender to God's will cost each of them dearly in terms of emotional suffering. (In Hannah's case, this meant the painful sorrow of separation from her own child. Samuel left home to begin his full-time training in the tabernacle when he was still a young toddler, at a time when most children still enjoy the comfort of their mothers' arms.)

A CHERISHED HOPE

Hannah was unique among the women we have studied so far because she was not in the genealogical line of the Messiah. But Hannah's famous dedicatory prayer, when she offered her son to God, is actually a prophetic paean to Israel's Messiah. Clearly, she cherished the very same messianic hope that framed the worldview of every one of the extraordinary women we are studying.

As a matter of fact, since Hannah is the last of the Old Testament women we'll be dealing with, it is worth mentioning how prominent the messianic expectation is in the Old Testament—not only in the lives of these few women, but throughout the law, the psalms, and the prophets (Luke 24:44). The theme runs like a brilliant scarlet thread woven into the tapestry of the Old Testament. Here and there, it comes boldly to the surface in explicit prophecies and promises, but it is usually concealed just underneath, where it remains a constant undertone—always discernible but seldom conspicuous, and never really very far from the center of the picture. It is the true foundation for every *other* theme in the Old Testament.

I especially love how the messianic hope comes right to the forefront whenever we consider the principal women of the Old Testament. The

the messianic hope in the OT

88

truth is, every truly righteous man and woman in the Old Testament shared the same fervent longing for the Messiah to come. He was the focus and the theme of all their future hopes.

In other words, Christ has *always* been the one true object of all saving faith—even in Old Testament times. Long before He was explicitly revealed in human flesh, the Redeemer was promised. Although the Old Testament saints' understanding of Him was dim and shadowy, the promised Redeemer truly was the focus of all their hopes for salvation. Job, whose story is one of the most ancient expressions of faith recorded in Scripture, gave this testimony at the lowest point of his worst troubles: "I know that my Redeemer lives, and He shall stand at last on the earth; and after my skin is destroyed, this I know, that in my flesh I shall see God, whom I shall see for myself, and my eyes shall behold, and not another. How my heart yearns within me!" (Job 19:25–27 NKJV). Job's faith even included the expectation of his own bodily resurrection!

Job

The faith of true believers has *always* had that Christ-centered perspective. No wonder the messianic expectation was so prominent in the hearts and minds of these extraordinary women. It was the very essence of the faith by which they laid hold of God's promises. It was therefore the key to everything that made them truly extraordinary!

A GODLY HERITAGE

Hannah was an obscure woman living in a remote part of Israel with her husband, Elkanah. Hannah and Elkanah made their home in the territory occupied by the tribe of Ephraim. First Samuel 1:1 lists Elkanah's great-great-grandfather, Zuph, as an "Ephraimite," but this clearly designates only the territory the family lived in, and not their line of descent. We know this because 1 Chronicles 6:22–27 gives a detailed genealogy for Elkanah, showing that he actually descended from Levi by way of Kohath.

The Kohathites were one of the three major lines in the tribe of Levi.

This was an important clan. Moses and Aaron were Kohathites, according to 1 Chronicles 6:2–3. The sons of Kohath were assigned responsibility for the most sacred furnishings of the tabernacle, including the ark of the covenant (Num. 3:30–31). When Israel moved camp from one place to another in the wilderness, it was the Kohathites' duty to disassemble the Holy of Holies and transport the ark and all the sacred utensils according to a strict procedure (4:4–16).

Kohathites

Once Israel occupied the Promised Land permanently and the tabernacle was finally situated at Shiloh, the Kohathites seem to have devoted themselves to other priestly functions—especially leading music, prayer, and praise in the tabernacle (1 Chron. 6:31–33). Thus one of Elkanah's close ancestors was known as "Heman the singer," according to verse 33.

The Levites were the only tribe in Israel allotted no independent territory of their own because they were the priestly tribe, and the Lord Himself was their inheritance (Num. 18:20). So when the land of Israel was divided and distributed according to the twelve other tribes, the Levites were scattered throughout the whole nation. They were given modest plots of pastureland and fields to cultivate in selected cities throughout Israel. Elkanah's ancestors, probably as far back as the earliest generation after the conquest of Canaan, had lived among the tribe of Ephraim. That's why Zuph (Elkanah's ancestor) is called an "Ephraimite," even though this was clearly a family of Kohathites, from the tribe of Levi.

serving at Shiloh

Men from the tribe of Levi took turns every year (for a few weeks at a time) serving in the tabernacle. In those days, the tabernacle was situated at Shiloh. Since the Levites had this duty to minister in the tabernacle, taking them away from their land and homes for an extended time each year, their income was supplemented with tithes collected from all Israel (Num. 18:24–32).

Hannah faithfully traveled with Elkanah to the tabernacle every year to worship and offer a sacrifice. Scripture portrays them as a devout family, yet living in a dismal period of Israel's history. The Bible reminds us that at the time Elkanah made regular trips to Shiloh to worship and offer his sacrifice, "the two sons of Eli, Hophni and Phinehas, the priests of the LORD, were there" (1 Sam. 1:3 NKJV).

Hophni and Phinehas were two of the *worst* priests we ever meet on the pages of Scripture. They were greedy men who illegally—and sometimes forcibly—took the best portions of people's offerings for themselves (1 Sam. 2:13–16). Worse yet, they used their position as priests to seduce young women (v. 22). They had, in effect, turned the tabernacle into a bawdy house, and they had formed a kind of priestly mafia, bullying worshipers and flagrantly showing contempt for God's law. The obvious result was that the people of Israel grew to abhor bringing their offerings to the Lord (v. 17). All the people of Israel were aware of what Hophni and Phinehas were doing, but their father Eli made only a half-hearted attempt to rebuke them, even though he was the high priest (v. 24).

Of course, the visible manifestation of God's glory that once resided over the ark of the covenant was long gone. The ark itself had come to mean little to the Israelites. Hophni and Phinehas treated it like a talisman. The low point came when they took it into battle against the Philistines, presuming it would guarantee Israel a victory. Instead, the Philistines soundly defeated Israel's army and captured the ark. The ark was never again returned to the tabernacle at Shiloh. (After its recovery from the Philistines, the ark remained in virtual neglect for about a hundred years in a private house in Kiriath-Jearim, until David retrieved it and brought it to Jerusalem in preparation for the temple Solomon would build there.)

The loss of the ark (1 Sam. 4:10–11) occurred just a few short years after Hannah is introduced to us in Scripture (1:2). It was the climactic and defining moment of that backslidden era. Incidentally, in that same battle in which the ark was captured, Hophni and Phinehas were killed. Eli fell over from shock as soon as he heard the news. He died too—from injuries sustained in that fall. Phinehas's wife delivered a child shortly after that, and she named him Ichabod, meaning "the glory has departed" (4:12–22 NKJV). It was an apt description of that whole era of Israel's history. This was indeed a time of great spiritual darkness.

In those dry and gloomy days, Hannah stood out as a ray of light. Not only was she the quintessential godly mother and wife, but in a spiritually cold generation she exemplified patience, prayerfulness, faith, meekness, submission, spiritual devotion, and motherly love.

A HOLY AMBITION

In spite of her gracious character, Hannah's home life was often troubled and sorrowful. Her husband was a bigamist. In the words of Scripture, "He had two wives: the name of one was Hannah, and the name of the other Peninnah. Peninnah had children, but Hannah had no children" (1 Sam. 1:2 NKJV). Obviously, this situation caused severe tension in the family. Peninnah—called Hannah's "rival" (v. 6 NKJV)—deliberately provoked her, goading her about the fact that the Lord had withheld children from her.

Elkanah preferred Hannah, whom he loved deeply, but that only magnified the bitter rivalry between the women. Such strife was an inevitable side effect of Elkanah's bigamy. Of course, one of the obvious reasons God designed marriage as a monogamous relationship in the first place was to avoid this kind of strife within families.

Hannah was in constant anguish because of her own infertility. She was further tormented by Peninnah's carping taunts. The burden and stress made life almost unbearable. Hannah wept bitterly, and she literally could not even eat at times (1:7). She longed to be a mother. This was her one ambition in life.

I am convinced it was no selfish aspiration. The way Hannah immediately dedicated her first son to the Lord and gave him over to serve in the tabernacle at such a young age demonstrates the purity of her motives.

motherhood

She understood that motherhood is the highest calling God can bestow on
any woman.

That is not to suggest, of course, that motherhood is the *only* proper
role for women. Scripture recognizes that it is God's will for some women
to remain single (1 Cor. 7:8–9). In the wisdom of His providence, He has
also ordained that some married women will remain perpetually childless
(see Psalm 127:3). A woman is by no means *required* to be a wife or a
mother before she can be useful in the Lord's service. Miriam (Moses' sister) and Deborah (who served as a judge and deliverer in Israel) are biblical examples of women whom God used mightily apart from marriage or
motherhood. (Deborah was married, but she gained renown in a role that
had nothing to do with being a wife or mother.)

Still, Scripture frequently portrays marriage as "the grace of life" (1 Pet.
3:7 NKJV) and motherhood as the *highest* calling any woman could ever be
summoned to. It is, after all, the one vocation that God uniquely designed
women to fulfill, and no man can ever intrude into the mother's role.
Perhaps you have already noticed how the glory and dignity of motherhood stood out in one way or another as a major theme in the life of every
woman we have dealt with so far. That is true of *most* of the key women
in Scripture. Scripture honors them for their faithfulness in their own
homes. Or, as in the case of Rahab and Ruth, we remember them because
by faith they were liberated from the bondage of the world and raised to
the more exalted role of wife and mother. Only rarely in Scripture were
women singled out and praised for exploits or careers outside the domestic realm. Honor and eminence for women in the Bible was nearly always
closely associated with home and family. Hannah understood that, and she
earnestly desired to enter into the noble role of a mother.

Of course, the Bible's exaltation of motherhood is often scorned by our
more "enlightened" age. In fact, in this generation, motherhood is frequently derided and belittled even in the name of "women's rights." But
it has been God's plan from the beginning that women should train and

nurture godly children and thus leave a powerful imprint on society through the home (1 Tim. 5:10; Titus 2:3–5). Hannah is a classic illustration of how that works. She is a reminder that mothers are the makers of men and the architects of the next generation. Her earnest prayer for a child was the beginning of a series of events that helped turn back the spiritual darkness and backsliding in Israel. She set in motion a chain of events that would ultimately usher in a profound spiritual awakening at the dawn of the Davidic dynasty.

We first encounter Hannah when Israel was in desperate need of a great leader and a great man. Hannah became the woman whom God used to help shape that man. Samuel proved to be the one man who could fill the leadership void. His character bore the clear stamp of his mother's influence, even though he left home at such an early age.

I believe Hannah's influence as a godly wife and mother is traceable to the three great loves of her life.

LOVE FOR HER HUSBAND

From the beginning of Scripture's account of her family, it is evident that Hannah had a deep love for Elkanah, as he did for her. When they made a peace offering to the Lord (a sacrifice in which the offerer roasted the sacrificial animal and partook of a feast unto the Lord), Elkanah gave portions to Peninnah and all her children, but he gave a double portion to Hannah because of his great love for her (1 Sam. 1:4–5). This was a public honor that he regularly and deliberately bestowed on her in the presence of others at a feast.

Obviously, Hannah's marriage was not a perfect one, chiefly because of the jealousy and rivalry her husband's polygamous marriage caused. Hannah seemed to be the first wife, since she is named first (v. 2). Apparently Elkanah later married Peninnah because of Hannah's barrenness. Remember, it was deemed vitally important in that culture to have children who could maintain the family inheritance and the family name. This was the same reason Abraham entered into a polygamous relationship with Hagar. It is undoubtedly the main reason we see so much polygamy in the Old Testament.

But Hannah's marriage, though marred by tensions, was solid. Elkanah obviously loved Hannah with a sincere affection, and he knew her love for him was reciprocal. In fact, he tried to comfort her by tenderly reminding her of his love for her: "Hannah, why do you weep? Why do you not eat? And why is your heart grieved? Am I not better to you than ten sons?" (v. 8 NKJV). This plea *did* help, at least for the moment, because Hannah immediately arose and ate, then went to the tabernacle (v. 9).

Hannah's love for her husband is the first key to understanding her profound influence as a mother. Contrary to popular opinion, the most important characteristic of a godly mother is not her relationship with her *children*. It is her love for her *husband*. The love between husband and wife is the real key to a thriving family. A healthy home environment cannot be built exclusively on the parents' love for their children. The properly situated family has *marriage* at the center; families shouldn't revolve around the children.

Furthermore, all parents need to heed this lesson: what you communicate to your children through your marital relationship will stay with them for the rest of their lives. By watching how mother and father treat one another, they will learn the most fundamental lessons of life—love, self-sacrifice, integrity, virtue, sin, sympathy, compassion, understanding, and forgiveness. Whatever you teach them about those things, right or wrong, is planted deep within their hearts.

That emphasis on the centrality of marriage was very evident between Elkanah and Hannah. With all their domestic issues, they nonetheless had a healthy marriage and an abiding love for one another. Their inability to have children together was like an open wound. But it was an experience that drew out of Elkanah tender expressions of love for his wife. And even in a home environment with a second wife and multiple children—a chaos created by the folly of Elkanah's bigamy and made even more dysfunctional by Peninnah's ill temperament—Hannah and Elkanah clearly loved one another deeply.

They worshiped God together, and they did so regularly. Verse 3 says, "This man went up from his city *yearly* to worship and sacrifice to the LORD of hosts in Shiloh" (NKJV). But that doesn't mean Hannah and Elkanah visited the tabernacle *only* once a year. All Israelite men were required to attend three annual feasts (Deut. 16:1–17). Most likely, Elkanah took his family with him on those journeys. They probably traveled to Shiloh together on other occasions too. (The journey from the family home in Ramathaim Zophim to Shiloh was a distance of about twenty-five miles along the edge of the Jordan Valley. The trip could easily be made in two days or less.) Worship seemed to have been a central aspect of Hannah and Elkanah's lives together. This was what kept their love for one another strong in the face of so much adversity.

It also explains the second reason why Hannah was such an influential mother. As much as she loved Elkanah, there was an even greater love that motivated her.

LOVE FOR HEAVEN

Hannah obviously had a deep and abiding love for God. Her spiritual passion was seen in the fervency of her prayer life. She was a devout woman whose affections were set on heavenly things, not on earthly things. Her desire for a child was no mere craving for self-gratification. It wasn't about her. It wasn't about getting what she wanted. It was about self-sacrifice—giving herself to that little life in order to give him back to the Lord. Centuries earlier, Jacob's wife Rachel prayed, "Give me children, or else I die!" (Gen. 30:1 NKJV). Hannah's prayer was more modest than that. She did not pray for "children," but for one son. She begged God for one son who would be fit to serve in the tabernacle. If God would give her that son, she would give him back to God. Hannah's actions proved that she wanted a child not for her own pleasure, but because she wanted to dedicate him to the Lord.

Naturally, then, the Lord was the One to whom she turned to plead her case. It was significant, I think, that despite the bitter agony Hannah suffered because of her childlessness, she never became a complainer or a nag. There's no suggestion that she ever grumbled against God or badgered her husband about her childlessness. Why should she whine to Elkanah? Children are an inheritance from the Lord (Ps. 127:3; Gen. 33:5). Hannah seems to have understood that, so she took her case straight to the Lord. Despite her disappointment and heartache, she remained faithful to YHWH. In fact, frustration seems to have turned her more and more *to* the Lord, not *away* from him. And she persisted in prayer.

That's a beautiful characteristic, and it was Hannah's distinctive virtue: constant, steadfast faith. First Samuel 1:12 speaks of her prayer as continual: "She *continued* praying before the LORD" (NKJV, emphasis added). She stayed before the Lord, even with a broken heart, pouring out tearful prayers. Her trials thus had the benefit of making her a woman of prayer. She truly exemplified what it meant to "pray without ceasing" (1 Thess. 5:17; Luke 18:1–8).

The value of persistent and passionate prayer is one of the central lessons from Hannah's life. Notice how the passion of her praying is described in 1 Samuel 1:10–11: "And she was in bitterness of soul, and prayed to the LORD and wept in anguish. *Then she made a vow* and said, 'O LORD of hosts, if You will indeed look on the affliction of Your maidservant and remember me, and not forget Your maidservant, but will give Your maidservant a male child, then I will give him to the LORD all the days of his life, and no razor shall come upon his head'" (NKJV, emphasis added).

There were two parts to Hannah's vow. One was the promise to give the child to the Lord. Subsequent events indicated that by this pledge she intended to devote him to full-time service in the tabernacle. The last part of Hannah's promise entailed a vow never to cut his hair. This was one of three provisions of the ancient Nazirite vow (Num. 6:1–9). While it was not clear whether Hannah's promise also entailed all the other provisions of the Nazirite vow, if it had, her son would have also been required to abstain from wine (or any product of grapes) and not come in contact with anything that would cause ceremonial defilement. These restrictions were signs of consecration to God.

Both parts of Hannah's vow consecrated her son for life to duties that normally would have been only temporary. Levites, as we have seen, took turns serving in the tabernacle. No one had the responsibility for life. Nazirite vows were usually only temporary too. Of course, God had expressly commanded Samson's mother to make him a Nazirite for life (Judg. 13:2–7). (Since Samson's mother had been barren before Samson was conceived, Hannah's knowledge of that history may be what prompted her to make this vow.) John the Baptist also seemed to have been under a similar lifelong vow (Luke 7:33). But normally such vows lasted a few weeks or years at the most.

Hannah obviously wanted her son to be a godly man, serving and glorifying the Lord all his life. These were not promises she made lightly, and when God finally answered her prayer, she did not recoil from the difficult duty her vow had placed on her as Samuel's mother.

The intensity of Hannah's prayer made her conspicuous in the tabernacle, especially in that backslidden era. She was so totally consumed by the passion of her prayer and so distraught with weeping (1 Sam. 1:10) that she caught the attention of the old priest, Eli. He had probably never witnessed more passionate, heartfelt praying, though he didn't even know it was that:

> And it happened, as she continued praying before the LORD, that Eli
> watched her mouth. Now Hannah spoke in her heart; only her lips moved,

but her voice was not heard. Therefore Eli thought she was drunk. So Eli said to her, "How long will you be drunk? Put your wine away from you!"

And Hannah answered and said, "No, my lord, I am a woman of sorrowful spirit. I have drunk neither wine nor intoxicating drink, but have poured out my soul before the LORD. Do not consider your maidservant a wicked woman, for out of the abundance of my complaint and grief I have spoken until now."

Then Eli answered and said, "Go in peace, and the God of Israel grant your petition which you have asked of Him." (1 Sam. 1:12–17 NKJV)

Eli's insensitive response was typical of him. It showed how utterly he lacked any sense of discernment or even basic courtesy. This is a large part of the explanation for why he was so incompetent in his roles as high priest to the nation and father to his own sons. His accusation against Hannah was the same accusation the unbelieving mob made against the disciples on the day of Pentecost (Acts 2:13). Eli evidently did not recognize that she was praying.

A couple of factors may have contributed to his confusion. In the first place, it was customary in Israel to pray aloud, not silently. Hannah seems to have understood that God sees right into the human heart. He knows our thoughts even before they become words; and He knows our words before they are formed on our lips (Ps. 139:1–4). Furthermore, we are taught in the New Testament that the Holy Spirit intercedes for us with groanings that can't even be uttered (Rom. 8:26). So there was no need for Hannah to pray aloud. She wasn't doing it for ceremony. She knew that the Lord knew her heart. By contrast, private prayer seemed to have been so foreign to Eli that he could not even recognize prayer when he saw it, unless it conformed to ceremonial customs.

A second thing that may have obscured Eli's discernment was the fact that his own sons were known to consort with loose women right there in the tabernacle (1 Sam. 2:22). Eli certainly did not approve of his sons' behavior, but he failed to take strong enough measures to keep it from happening. Apparently he was more accustomed to seeing immoral women at the tabernacle than godly ones, so he may have assumed that Hannah was one of those women.

His rebuke was nonetheless foolish and uncalled for. Drunkenness usually makes people noisy and boisterous. Hannah was silent and keeping completely to herself. There was no reason whatsoever for Eli to scold her like that.

Hannah answered with characteristic grace and humility. Of course, she was horrified by his accusation and denied it with a clear tone of chagrin. She explained that she was merely pouring out her heart in sorrow. She didn't tell Eli the reason for her sorrow. There was no need for that. She understood that only God could answer her prayer; that was why her prayers had been silent in the first place.

For his part, Eli quickly changed his tone. He must have been somewhat embarrassed and chastened to learn how badly he had misjudged this poor woman. Because of that, he blessed her and called on the Lord to grant her petition.

Hannah's final response to Eli revealed another of her positive spiritual traits. "And she said, 'Let your maidservant find favor in your sight.' So the woman went her way and ate, and her face was no longer sad" (1:18 NKJV). Hannah cast her whole burden upon the Lord and left her sense of frustration there at the altar. She did what she had come to the tabernacle to do. She had brought her case before the Lord. Now she was content to leave the matter in His hands.

That demonstrates how genuine and patient her faith truly was. Scripture says, "Cast your burden on the LORD, and He shall sustain you" (Ps. 55:22 NKJV). Some people will pray, "O God, here's my problem," and then leave His presence in complete doubt and frustration, still shouldering the same burden they originally brought before the Lord, not really trusting Him to sustain them. Hannah truly laid her troubles in the lap of the Lord, totally confident that He would answer her in accord for what was best for her. There's a real humility in that kind of faith, as the apostle Peter noted: "Humble yourselves under the mighty hand of God, that He may exalt you in due time, casting all your care upon Him, for He cares for you" (1 Peter 5:6–7 NKJV).

When God finally *did* answer Hannah's prayer by giving her the son she had asked for, her thankful soul responded with a pure, unbroken stream of praise. Her words, recorded for us in 1 Samuel 2:1–10, are a masterpiece. In the chapter that follows, we'll examine Mary's Magnificat, which is a close parallel to this passage both in its style and its substance:

And Hannah prayed and said:

"My heart rejoices in the LORD;
My horn is exalted in the LORD.
I smile at my enemies,
Because I rejoice in Your salvation.

"No one is holy like the LORD,
For there is none besides You,
Nor is there any rock like our God.

"Talk no more so very proudly;
Let no arrogance come from your mouth,
For the LORD is the God of knowledge;
And by Him actions are weighed.

"The bows of the mighty men are broken,
And those who stumbled are girded with strength.
Those who were full have hired themselves out for bread,
And the hungry have ceased to hunger.
Even the barren has borne seven,

And she who has many children has become feeble.

"The LORD kills and makes alive;
He brings down to the grave and brings up.
The LORD makes poor and makes rich;
He brings low and lifts up.
He raises the poor from the dust
And lifts the beggar from the ash heap,
To set them among princes
And make them inherit the throne of glory.

"For the pillars of the earth are the Lord's,
And He has set the world upon them.
He will guard the feet of His saints,
But the wicked shall be silent in darkness.

"For by strength no man shall prevail.
The adversaries of the LORD shall be broken in pieces;
From heaven He will thunder against them.
The LORD will judge the ends of the earth.

"He will give strength to His king,
And exalt the horn of His anointed." (NKJV)

There's enough solid content in that brief thanksgiving anthem that we could spend many pages analyzing it. If it were given to me as a text to preach on, I would undoubtedly have to preach a series of several sermons just to unpack its prophetic and doctrinal significance completely. Obviously, we don't have enough space for that kind of thorough study of Hannah's hymn of praise. But even the briefest overview reveals how thoroughly familiar Hannah was with the deep things of God.

She acknowledged, for example, God's holiness, His goodness, His sovereignty, His power, and His wisdom. She worshiped Him as Savior, as Creator, and as sovereign judge. She acknowledged the fallenness and depravity of human nature, as well as the folly of unbelief and rebellion. In short, her few stanzas were a masterpiece of theological understanding.

But this was not mere academic theology. Hannah spoke about God from her own intimate knowledge of Him. Her words of praise were filled with love and wonder. That love for God, and a love for all things heavenly, was one of the keys to Hannah's lasting influence as a mother.

LOVE FOR HER HOME

A third major characteristic of Hannah was her devotion to home and family. We see evidence of this from the beginning, in her love for Elkanah and his love for her. We see it in the way she rose above the petty strife and feuding Peninnah deliberately tried to sow within her own household with no other intention than to exasperate Hannah. We see it again in Hannah's intense longing to be a mother. We see it best in how committed she was to her child in his infancy.

When Hannah and Elkanah returned home after her encounter with Eli in the tabernacle, Scripture says, "Elkanah knew Hannah his wife, and the LORD remembered her. So it came to pass in the process of time that Hannah conceived and bore a son" (1:19–20 NKJV). She named him Samuel, but the meaning of *Samuel* is not entirely clear. It could literally be translated "name of God." Some commentators suggest it could mean "asked from God," and others say "heard by God." In Hebrew, the name is very similar to Ishmael, which means, "God shall hear." Whatever the actual significance of the name, the essence of what it meant to Hannah is clear. Samuel was a living answer to prayer and a reminder that God had heard what she asked and granted her heart's desire.

Hannah devoted herself solely to Samuel's care for the next few years. When the time came to make the first trip to Shiloh after the baby's birth,

Hannah told her husband she planned to stay at home with Samuel until he was weaned. "Then," she said, "I will take him, that he may appear before the LORD and remain there forever" (v. 22 NKJV).

She knew her time with Samuel would be short. Mothers in that culture nursed their children for about three years. She would care for him during his most formative years, while he learned to walk and talk. As soon as he was weaned, though, she was determined to fulfill her vow.

In the meantime, she would be a fixture in his life. She became the very model of a stay-at-home mom. No mother was ever more devoted to home and child. She had important work to do—nurturing him, caring for him, and helping him learn the most basic truths of life and wisdom. She taught him his first lessons about YHWH. She made her home an environment where he could learn and grow in safety. And she carefully directed the course of his learning and helped shape his interests.

Hannah seemed to understand how vital those early years are, when 90 percent of personality is formed. "Train up a child in the way he should go, and when he is old he will not depart from it" (Prov. 22:6 NKJV). She prepared Samuel in those formative years for a lifetime of service to God— the high calling to which she had consecrated him before he was ever born. History tells us that she did her job well. Samuel, obviously a precocious child, grew in wisdom and understanding. Those early years set a course for his life from which he never deviated. The only blot on his record came in his old age, when he made his sons judges and they perverted justice (1 Sam. 8:1–3). Samuel's own failure as a father was the one aspect of his life that obviously owed more to the influence of Eli, the old priest, than to the example of Hannah.

Hannah's devotion to home and motherhood was exemplary in every way. Her devotion to her son in those early years makes her ultimate willingness to hand Samuel over to a life of service in the tabernacle seem all the more remarkable. It must have been intensely painful for her to send him off at such a tender age. In effect, the tabernacle became his boarding school and Eli his tutor. But it is apparent that Hannah's influence on Samuel remained far more of a guiding force in his life than the spiritually feeble example of Eli.

No doubt Hannah kept as close to Samuel as the arrangement would allow. She and Elkanah naturally would have increased their visits to Shiloh in light of Hannah's intense love for Samuel. It seems safe to surmise that they probably extended the duration of each visit too. Scripture says she "used to make him a little robe, and bring it to him year by year when she came up with her husband to offer the yearly sacrifice" (1 Sam. 2:19 NKJV). Again, "yearly" in this case doesn't mean "just once a year." It speaks of the regularity and faithfulness of their visits. Hannah thus continued to exercise a strong maternal influence on Samuel throughout all his formative years.

Scripture says God blessed Hannah with five more children—three sons and two daughters (v. 21). Her home and family life became rich and full. She was blessed by God to be allowed to achieve every ambition she had ever longed to fulfill. Her love for heaven, husband, and home are still the true priorities for every godly wife and mother. Her extraordinary life stands as a wonderful example to women today who want their homes to be places where God is honored, even in the midst of a dark and sinful culture. Hannah showed us what the Lord can do through one woman totally and unreservedly devoted to Him.

May her tribe increase.

6

MARY: BLESSED AMONG WOMEN

❦

The virgin's name was Mary. And having come in, the angel said to her, "Rejoice, highly favored one, the Lord is with you; blessed are you among women!"

Luke 1:27–28 NKJV

Of all the extraordinary women in Scripture, one stands out above all others as the most blessed, most highly favored by God, and most universally admired by women. Indeed, no woman is more truly remarkable than Mary. She was the one sovereignly chosen by God—from among all the women who have ever been born—to be the singular instrument through which He would at last bring the Messiah into the world.

Mary herself testified that all generations would regard her as profoundly blessed by God (Luke 1:48). This was not because she believed herself to be any kind of saintly superhuman, but because she was given such remarkable grace and privilege.

While acknowledging that Mary was the most extraordinary of women, it is appropriate to inject a word of caution against the common tendency to elevate her *too much*. She was, after all, a woman—not a demigoddess or a quasi-deiform creature who somehow transcended the rest of her race. The point of her "blessedness" is certainly not that we should think of her as someone to whom we can appeal for blessing; but rather that she herself was supremely blessed by God. She is never portrayed in Scripture as a source or dispenser of grace, but is herself the recipient of God's blessing. Her Son, not Mary herself, is the fountain of grace (Ps. 72:17). *He* is the long-awaited Seed of Abraham of whom the covenant promise spoke: "In your seed all the nations of the earth shall be blessed" (Gen. 22:18 NKJV).

Various extrabiblical religious traditions and many superstitious minds have beatified Mary beyond what is reasonable, making her an object of religious veneration, imputing to her various titles and attributes that belong to God alone. A long tradition of overzealous souls throughout history have wrongly exalted her to godlike status. Unfortunately, even in our era, Mary, not Christ, is the central focus of worship and religious affection for millions. They think of her as more approachable and more sympathetic than Christ. They revere her as the perfect Madonna, supposedly untouched by original sin, a perpetual virgin, and even co-redemptrix with Christ Himself. Catholic dogma teaches that she was taken bodily to heaven, where she was crowned "Queen of Heaven." Her role today, according to Catholic legend, is mediatory and intercessory. Therefore, multitudes direct their prayers to her instead of to God alone—as if Mary were omnipresent and omniscient.

As a matter of fact, many people superstitiously imagine that Mary regularly appears in various apparitions here and there, and some even claim that she delivers prophecies to the world through such means. This extreme gullibility about apparitions of Mary sometimes rises to almost comical proportions. In November 2004, a stale grilled-cheese sandwich sold for $28,000 in an eBay auction because the sandwich purportedly had an image of Mary supernaturally etched in the burn marks of the toast. A few months later, thousands of worshipers in Chicago built a makeshift shrine to Mary in the walkway of a freeway underpass because someone claimed to see an image of her in salt stains on the concrete wall of the abutment.

No less than Pope John Paul II declared his total devotion to Mary. He dedicated his whole pontificate to her and had an M for Mary embroidered in all his papal garments. He prayed to her, credited her with saving his life, and even left the care of the Roman Catholic Church to her in his will. Rome has long fostered the cult of Marian devotion, and superstition about Mary is more popular today than it has ever been. So much homage is paid to Mary in Catholic churches around the world that the centrality and supremacy of Christ is often utterly obscured by the adoration of His mother.

All such veneration of Mary is entirely without biblical warrant. In fact, it is completely *contrary* to what Scripture expressly teaches (Rev. 19:10). But the tendency to make Mary an object of worship is nothing new. Even during Jesus' earthly ministry, for example, there were those who showed undue reverence to Mary because of her role as His mother. On one occasion, Scripture says, a woman in the crowd raised her voice and said to Jesus, "Blessed is the womb that bore You, and the breasts at which You nursed."

His reply was a rebuke: "On the contrary, blessed are those who hear the word of God, and observe it" (Luke 11:27–28 NASB).

Mary herself was a humble soul who maintained a consistently low profile in the gospel accounts of Jesus' life. Scripture expressly debunks some of the main legends about her. The idea that she remained a perpetual virgin, for example, is impossible to reconcile with the fact that Jesus had half-brothers who are named in Scripture alongside both Joseph and Mary as their parents: "Is this not the carpenter's son? Is not His mother called Mary? And His brothers James, Joses, Simon, and Judas?" (Matt. 13:55 NKJV). Matthew 1:25 furthermore says that Joseph abstained from sexual relations with Mary only "till she had brought forth her firstborn Son" (NKJV). On any natural reading of the plain sense of Scripture, it is impossible to support the idea of Mary's perpetual virginity.

Mary's immaculate conception and her supposed sinlessness are likewise without any scriptural foundation whatsoever. The opening stanza of Mary's Magnificat speaks of God as her "Savior," thus giving implicit testimony from Mary's own lips that she needed redemption. In such a biblical context, that could refer only to salvation from sin. Mary was in effect confessing her own sinfulness.

In fact, far from portraying Mary with a halo and a seraphic stare on her face, Scripture reveals her as an average young girl of common means from a peasants' town in a poor region of Israel, betrothed to a working-class fiancé who earned his living as a carpenter. If you had met Mary before her firstborn Son was miraculously conceived, you might not have noticed her at all. She could hardly have been more plain and unassuming. From everything we know of her background and social standing, not much about her life or her experience so far would be deemed very extraordinary.

MARY'S HERITAGE

Mary did have some illustrious ancestors, though. Luke gave us her gene-alogy in detail (Luke 3:23–38). Matthew, likewise, listed Joseph's (Matt. 1:1–16). Both Joseph and Mary descended from David. Therefore, prior to David, they shared the same genealogy. Mary's branch of David's family tree can be traced through David's son named Nathan, while Joseph's branch is the royal line, through Solomon. In light of this, Christ inherited David's throne through his stepfather. It was his birthright as a firstborn son. Jesus' blood relationship to David, however, came through Mary who descended from an otherwise inconsequential branch of David's family.

Remember that Matthew included several women in the genealogy of Christ. Since all those women came between Abraham and David, all of them were ancestors of both Joseph and Mary—including Rahab and Ruth. Of course, Sarah (though unnamed in the New Testament genealo-gies) was the wife of Abraham and the mother of Isaac. And Eve was the mother of all living. Therefore, with the single exception of Hannah, every one of the extraordinary women we have examined so far was an ancestor of Mary. She seems to have inherited the best traits of all of them. (As we're going to see, she also reflected the best aspects of Hannah's character.) Most significant of all, her faith was an extraordinary example of the kind of faith Jesus blessed. She was sincere, earnestly worshipful, childlike in her trust of the Lord, and utterly dependent on Him.

Then she found herself unexpectedly thrust into the very role each one of her illustrious ancestors had longed to fulfill. She would become the mother of the promised Redeemer.

THE ANNOUNCEMENT THAT CHANGED HER LIFE

When we first meet Mary in Luke's gospel, it is on the occasion when an archangel appeared to her suddenly and without fanfare to disclose to her God's wonderful plan. Scripture says, simply, "The angel Gabriel was sent by God to a city of Galilee named Nazareth, to a virgin betrothed to a man whose name was Joseph, of the house of David. The virgin's name was Mary" (Luke 1:26–27 NKJV).

Mary is the equivalent of the Hebrew "Miriam." The name may be derived from the Hebrew word for "bitter." (As we saw in the story of Ruth, her mother-in-law Naomi referred to herself as "Mara," a reference to the bitterness of her trials.) Mary's young life may well have been filled with bitter hardships. Her hometown was a forlorn community in a poor district of Galilee. Nazareth, you may recall, famously bore the brunt of at least one future disciple's disdain. When Philip told Nathanael that he had found the Messiah and the Anointed One was a Galilean from Nazareth, Nathanael sneered, "Can anything good come out of Nazareth?" (John 1:45–46 NKJV). Mary had lived there all her life, in a community where, frankly, good things probably were pretty scarce.

Other details about Mary's background can be gleaned here and there in Scripture. She had a sister, according to John 19:25. There's not enough data in the text to identify accurately who the sister was, but Mary's sister was herself obviously a close enough disciple of Jesus to be present with the other faithful women at the crucifixion. Mary was also a close relative of Elizabeth, mother of John the Baptist (Luke 1:36). The nature of that relationship isn't specifically described. They might have been cousins, or Elizabeth might have been Mary's aunt. Luke's account describes Elizabeth as already "in her old age." Mary, on the other hand, seems to have been quite young.

In fact, at the time of the Annunciation, Mary was probably still a teenager. It was customary for girls in that culture to be betrothed while they were still as young as thirteen years of age. Marriages were ordinarily arranged by the bridegroom or his parents through the girl's father. Mary was betrothed to Joseph, about whom we know next to nothing—except that he was a carpenter (Mark 6:3) and a righteous man (Matt. 1:19).

Scripture is very clear in teaching that Mary was still a virgin when Jesus was miraculously conceived in her womb. Luke 1:27 twice calls her a virgin, using a Greek term that allows for no subtle nuance of meaning. The clear claim of Scripture, and Mary's own testimony, is that she had never been physically intimate with any man. Her betrothal to Joseph was a legal engagement known as *kiddushin,* which in that culture typically lasted a full year. *Kiddushin* was legally as binding as marriage itself. The couple were deemed husband and wife, and only a legal divorce could dissolve the marriage contract (Matt. 1:19). But during this time, the couple lived separately from one another and had no physical relations whatsoever. One of the main points of *kiddushin* was to demonstrate the fidelity of both partners.

When the angel appeared to Mary, she was already formally bound to Joseph by *kiddushin.* Luke 1:28–35 describes Mary's encounter with the angel:

> *And having come in, the angel said to her, "Rejoice, highly favored one, the Lord is with you; blessed are you among women!"*

But when she saw him, she was troubled at his saying, and considered what manner of greeting this was.

Then the angel said to her, "Do not be afraid, Mary, for you have found favor with God. And behold, you will conceive in your womb and bring forth a Son, and shall call His name JESUS. He will be great, and will be called the Son of the Highest; and the Lord God will give Him the throne of His father David. And He will reign over the house of Jacob forever, and of His kingdom there will be no end."

Then Mary said to the angel, "How can this be, since I do not know a man?"

And the angel answered and said to her, "The Holy Spirit will come upon you, and the power of the Highest will overshadow you; therefore, also, that Holy One who is to be born will be called the Son of God." (NKJV)

We have seen throughout this book how numerous godly women in Mary's ancestry, going all the way back to Eve, had fostered the hope of being the one through whom the Redeemer would come. But the privilege came at a high cost to Mary personally, because it carried the stigma of an unwed pregnancy. Although she had remained totally and completely chaste, the world was bound to think otherwise. Even Joseph assumed the worst. We can only imagine how his heart sank when he learned that Mary was pregnant, and he knew he was not the father. His inclination was to divorce her quietly. He was a righteous man and loved her, so Scripture says he was not willing to make a public example of her, but he was so shaken by the news of her pregnancy that at first he saw no option but divorce. Then an angel appeared to him in a dream and reassured him: "Joseph, son of David, do not be afraid to take to you Mary your wife, for that which is conceived in her is of the Holy Spirit. And she will bring forth a Son, and you shall call His name JESUS, for He will save His people from their sins" (Matt. 1:20–21 NKJV).

Common sense suggests that Mary must have anticipated all these difficulties the moment the angel told her she would conceive a child. Her joy and amazement at learning that she would be the mother of the Redeemer might therefore have been tempered significantly at the horror of the scandal that awaited her. Still, knowing the cost and weighing it against the immense privilege of becoming the mother of the Christ, Mary surrendered herself unconditionally, saying simply, "Behold the maidservant of the Lord! Let it be to me according to your word" (Luke 1:38 NKJV).

There's no evidence that Mary ever brooded over the effects her pregnancy would have on her reputation. She instantly, humbly, and joyfully submitted to God's will without further doubt or question. She could hardly have had a more godly response to the announcement of Jesus' birth. It demonstrated that she was a young woman of mature faith and one who was a worshiper of the true God. Her great joy over the Lord's plan for her would soon be very evident.

MARY'S RESPONSE OF WORSHIP

Mary, filled with joy and bubbling over with praise, hurried to the hill country to visit her beloved relative, Elizabeth. There's no suggestion that Mary was fleeing the shame of her premature pregnancy. It seems she simply wanted a kindred spirit to share her heart with. The angel had explicitly informed Mary about Elizabeth's pregnancy. So it was natural for her to seek out a close relative who was both a strong believer and also expecting her first son by a miraculous birth, announced by an angel (Luke 1:13–19). While Elizabeth was much older, maybe even in her eighties, and had always been unable to conceive, and Mary was at the beginning of life—both had been supernaturally blessed by God to conceive. It was a perfect situation for the two women to spend time rejoicing together in the Lord's goodness to both of them.

Elizabeth's immediate response to the sound of Mary's voice gave Mary independent confirmation of all that the angel had told her. Scripture says,

> *It happened, when Elizabeth heard the greeting of Mary, that the babe leaped in her womb; and Elizabeth was filled with the Holy Spirit. Then she spoke out with a loud voice and said, "Blessed are you among women, and blessed is the fruit of your womb! But why is this granted to me, that the mother of my Lord should come to me? For indeed, as soon as the voice of your greeting sounded in my ears, the babe leaped in my womb for joy. Blessed is she who believed, for there will be a fulfillment of those things which were told her from the Lord."* (Luke 1:41–45 NKJV)

Elizabeth's message was prophetic, of course, and Mary instantly understood that. Mary had learned from an angel about Elizabeth's pregnancy. Nothing indicates that Mary had sent word of her own circumstances ahead to Elizabeth. Indeed, Mary's sudden arrival had all the hallmarks of a surprise to her relative. Elizabeth's knowledge of Mary's pregnancy, therefore, seems to have come to her by revelation, in the prophecy she uttered when the Holy Spirit suddenly filled her.

Mary replied with prophetic words of her own. Her saying is known as the Magnificat (Latin for the first word of Mary's outpouring of praise). It is really a hymn about the incarnation. Without question, it is a song of unspeakable joy and the most magnificent psalm of worship in the New Testament. It is the equal of any Old Testament psalm, and as we have noted before, it bears a strong resemblance to Hannah's famous hymn of praise for the birth of Samuel. It is filled with messianic hope, scriptural language, and references to the Abrahamic covenant:

> *My soul magnifies the Lord,*
> *And my spirit has rejoiced in God my Savior.*

115

For He has regarded the lowly state of His maidservant;
For behold, henceforth all generations will call me blessed.
For He who is mighty has done great things for me,
And holy is His name.
And His mercy is on those who fear Him
From generation to generation.
He has shown strength with His arm;
He has scattered the proud in the imagination of their hearts.
He has put down the mighty from their thrones,
And exalted the lowly.
He has filled the hungry with good things,
And the rich He has sent away empty.
He has helped His servant Israel,
In remembrance of His mercy,
As He spoke to our fathers,
To Abraham and to his seed forever. (Luke 1:46–55 NKJV)

[handwritten marginalia: Mary is age 13 to 16]

It is clear that Mary's young heart and mind were already thoroughly saturated with the Word of God. She included not only echoes of two of Hannah's prayers (1 Sam. 1:11; 2:1–10), but also several other allusions to the law, the psalms, and the prophets:

Luke 1 (NKJV)	Old Testament (NKJV)
• "My soul magnifies the Lord" (46).	• "My heart rejoices in the Lord" (1 Sam. 2:1). • "My soul shall make its boast in the Lord" (Ps. 34:2). • "My soul shall be joyful in the Lord" (Ps. 35:9). • "I will greatly rejoice in the Lord, my soul shall be joyful in my God" (Isa. 61:10).

Luke 1 (NKJV)	Old Testament (NKJV)
• "And my spirit has rejoiced in God my Savior" (47).	• "God is my salvation" (Isa. 12:2). • "There is no other God besides Me, a just God and a Savior" (Isa. 45:21).
• "For He has regarded the lowly state of His maidservant" (48).	• "If You will indeed look on the affliction of Your maidservant and remember me, and not forget Your maidservant" (1 Sam. 1:11). • "He shall regard the prayer of the destitute, and shall not despise their prayer" (Ps. 102:17). • "Who remembered us in our lowly state, for His mercy endures forever" (Ps. 136:23).
• "For behold, henceforth all generations will call me blessed" (48).	• "Then Leah said, 'I am happy, for the daughters will call me blessed'" (Gen. 30:13). • "And all nations will call you blessed" (Mal. 3:12).
• "For He who is mighty has done great things for me" (49). • "And holy is His name" (49).	• "Your righteousness, O God, is very high, You who have done great things" (Ps. 71:19). • "The Lord has done great things for us, and we are glad" (Ps. 126:3). • "No one is holy like the Lord" (1 Sam. 2:2). • "Holy and awesome is His name" (Ps. 111:9). • "The High and Lofty One Who inhabits eternity, whose name is Holy" (Isa. 57:15).
• "And His mercy is on them who fear Him from generation to generation" (50).	• "So great is His mercy toward those who fear Him" (Ps. 103:11). • "The mercy of the Lord is from everlasting to everlasting on those who fear Him, and His righteousness to children's children" (Ps. 103:17).

MARY

Luke 1 (NKJV)	Old Testament (NKJV)
	• "My righteousness will be forever, and My salvation from generation to generation" (Isa. 51:8).
• "He has shown strength with His arm" (51).	• "You have a mighty arm; strong is Your hand, and high is Your right hand" (Ps. 89:13). • "He has done marvelous things; His right hand and His holy arm have gained Him the victory" (Ps. 98:1). • "The Lord has made bare His holy arm in the eyes of all the nations" (Isa. 52:10).
• "He has scattered the proud in the imagination of their hearts" (51).	• "You have scattered Your enemies with Your mighty arm" (Ps. 89:10). • "The imagination of man's heart is evil from his youth" (Gen. 8:21).
• "He has put down the mighty from their thrones, and exalted the lowly" (52).	• "The Lord kills and makes alive; He brings down to the grave and brings up. The Lord makes poor and makes rich; He brings low and lifts up. He raises the poor from the dust and lifts the beggar from the ash heap, to set them among princes and make them inherit the throne of glory" (1 Sam. 2:6–8). • "He breaks in pieces mighty men without inquiry, and sets others in their place" (Job 34:24).
• "He has filled the hungry with good things; and the rich He has sent away empty" (53).	• "He satisfies the longing soul, and fills the hungry soul with goodness" (Ps. 107:9).

Luke 1 (NKJV)	Old Testament (NKJV)
• "He has helped His servant Israel, in remembrance of His mercy, as He spoke to our fathers, to Abraham and to his seed forever" (54–55).	• "He has remembered His mercy and His fulness to the house of Israel" (Ps. 98:3). • "O Israel, you will not be forgotten by Me!" (Isa. 44:21). • "You will give truth to Jacob and mercy to Abraham, which You have sworn to our fathers from days of old" (Mic. 7:20). • "O seed of Abraham . . . He remembers His covenant forever, the word which He commanded, for a thousand generations, the covenant which He made with Abraham" (Ps. 105:6–9).

Those who channel their religious energies into the veneration of Mary would do well to learn from the example of Mary herself. God is the *only* One she magnified. Notice how she praised the glory and majesty of God while repeatedly acknowledging her own lowliness. She took no credit for anything good in herself. But she praised the Lord for His attributes, naming some of the chief ones specifically, including His power, His mercy, and His holiness. She freely confessed God as the one who had done great things for her, and not vice versa. The song is all about *God's* greatness, *His* glory, the strength of *His* arm, and *His* faithfulness across the generations.

Mary's worship was clearly from the heart. She was plainly consumed by the wonder of His grace to her. She seemed amazed that an absolutely holy God would do such great things for one as undeserving as she. This was not the prayer of one who claimed to be conceived immaculately, without the corruption of original sin. It was, on the contrary, the glad rejoicing of one who knew God intimately as her *Savior.* She could celebrate the fact that God's mercy is on those who fear Him, because she herself feared God and had received His mercy. And she knew firsthand how God exalts the lowly and fills the hungry with good things, because she herself was a humble sinner who had hungered and thirsted after righteousness, and was filled.

It was customary in Jewish prayers to recite God's past faithfulness to His people (Ex. 15; Judg. 5; Pss. 68; 78; 104; 105; 114; 135; 136; 145; and Hab. 3). Mary followed that convention here in abbreviated fashion. She recalled how God had helped Israel, in fulfillment of all His promises. Now her own child would be the living fulfillment of God's saving promise. No wonder Mary's heart overflowed with such praise.

HER RELATIONSHIP TO HER SON

Throughout Christ's earthly ministry, Mary appeared in only three scenes. On two of those occasions, Jesus Himself explicitly repudiated the notion that her earthly authority over Him as His mother entitled her to manage any aspect of His saving work. He did this without showing her the least bit of disrespect, of course, but He nonetheless clearly and completely disclaimed the idea that Mary was in any sense a mediator of His grace.

The first of these occasions was during the wedding at Cana, when Jesus performed His first miracle. The apostle John recorded what happened: "When they ran out of wine, the mother of Jesus said to Him, 'They have no wine'" (John 2:3 NKJV). The host at the wedding was undoubtedly a close family friend whom Mary cared a great deal for. (Notice how verse 1 says "the mother of Jesus was *there*"; but verse 2 says, "Jesus and His disciples were *invited*." Mary was evidently helping to coordinate the reception for her friend. Hence, she was one of the first to see that the wine supply was not going to be enough.) Mary also knew full well that Christ had the means to solve this embarrassing social dilemma, and she was subtly asking Him to do something about it. Whether she anticipated the kind of miracle He performed is not clear. She might have simply been prodding Him to make a suitable announcement and help cover the embarrassment for the hosts. Or, as it seems likely, she fully understood that He was the Prophet whom Moses foretold, and she was expecting Him, like Moses had so often done, to work a miracle that would supply what was lacking. She made no overt request, but her meaning was obviously plain to her Son.

For His part, Jesus had every intention of miraculously replenishing the wine, because that is what He subsequently did. He was never prone to vacillate, hesitate, or change His mind (Heb. 13:8). The fact that He ultimately performed the miracle is proof that He *planned* to do it.

Yet Scripture suggests His reply to Mary was somewhat terse. He was just as direct with Mary as she had been subtle with Him: "Jesus said to her, 'Woman, what does your concern have to do with Me? My hour has not yet come'" (John 2:4 NKJV). He was not being rude, and nothing suggests that Mary was in any way grieved or offended by His reply. "Woman" was a typical formal address in that culture. Again, it was curt without being impertinent. But there's no escaping the mild rebuke in His words and in His tone. The question, "What does your concern have to do with Me?" is a challenge seen several times in Scripture (Judg. 11:12; 2 Sam. 16:10; Ezra 4:2–3; Matt. 8:29). It conveyed a clear tone of displeasure and strong admonishment. Still, there's no suggestion that Mary took this as an affront. *His* intent was not to wound, but to correct and instruct.

Mary may have recalled a similar incident years before. As a young boy just entering young adulthood, Jesus was separated from His parents at the temple. After a frantic search, they found Him, and Mary mildly scolded Him for allowing them to be worried. He replied, with what appears to be genuine amazement, "Why did you seek Me? Did you not know that I must be about My Father's business?" (Luke 2:49 NKJV). He was, in effect, disclaiming any notion that His earthly father's parental interests could ever override the higher authority of His heavenly Father.

Here, at the Cana wedding, His message to Mary was similar. In spiritual matters, her earthly role as His mother did not give her any right to attempt to manage His mission as it pertained to fulfilling the Father's will on the Father's timetable. As a man, He was her Son. But as God, He was her Lord. It was not her business to command Him in spiritual matters. The way He spoke to her simply reminded her of that fact without showing her any real disrespect.

Then He turned the water to wine.

After that, Mary always remained in the background. She never sought or accepted the kind of preeminence so many seem determined to try to thrust on her. She never again attempted to intercede with Him for miracles, special favors, or other blessings on behalf of her friends, her relatives, or anyone else. It is only sheer folly that causes so many to imagine she has now usurped that role from her position in heaven.

Mary appeared again during Jesus' earthly ministry when the throngs who clamored for miracles from Christ had become larger than ever. Mark records that the demands of Jesus' ministry were such that He didn't even have time to eat (Mark 3:20). Jesus' own close family members began to be concerned for His safety, and they concluded (wrongly, of course) that He was beside Himself (v. 21). Scripture says they went to Him intending to physically pull Him away from the crowds and the heavy demands that they were making on Him.

Meanwhile, some scribes came from Jerusalem and accused Jesus of casting out demons in the power of Beelzebub (v. 22). Mark painted a vivid picture of chaos, opposition, and vast multitudes of needy people all pressing in on Jesus. It was into this context that His immediate family members came, seeking to get Him away from the multitudes for His own safety and sanity's sake. Mark 3:31–35 tells what happened:

Then His brothers and His mother came, and standing outside they sent to Him, calling Him. And a multitude was sitting around Him; and they said to Him, "Look, Your mother and Your brothers are outside seeking You."

*But He answered them, saying, "Who is My mother, or My brothers?" And He looked around in a circle at those who sat about Him, and said, "Here are My mother and My brothers! For whoever does the will of God is My brother and My sister and mother." (*NKJV*)*

Jesus sent the same message again. As far as His spiritual work was concerned, His earthly relatives had no more claim on Him than anyone else. He certainly did not set Mary on any exalted plane above His other disciples. He knew better than she did the limits of His human strength. He would not, even at her urging, leave what He was doing. He would not be interrupted or allow Himself to be sidetracked, even by her sincere maternal concern. As always, He must be about His *Father's* business, and she did not need to be consulted for that.

Once again, however, we see Mary learning to submit to Him as her Lord, rather than trying to control Him as His mother. She became one of His faithful disciples. She seems to have come to grips with the reality that He had work to do, and she could not direct it. She ultimately followed Him all the way to the cross, and on that dark afternoon when He died, she was standing nearby with a group of women, watching in grief and horror. The crucifixion was the third and final time Mary appeared alongside Jesus during the years of His public ministry.

THE SWORD THAT PIERCED HER SOUL

Mary had probably always had an inkling that this day would come. She had surely heard Jesus speak (as He did often) of His own death. As a matter of fact, the cloud of this inevitable reality had probably hung over

Mary's mind since Jesus' infancy. It was no doubt one of the things she kept and pondered in her heart (Luke 2:19, 51). Luke's gospel recounts how the first hint of impending tragedy crept into Mary's consciousness.

When Jesus was yet a newborn infant, His earthly parents took Him to the temple to dedicate Him to the Lord in accordance with the instructions of Exodus 13:2, 13: "Consecrate to Me all the firstborn, whatever opens the womb among the children of Israel . . . All the firstborn of man among your sons you shall redeem" (NKJV). Joseph and Mary came with a sacrifice of two turtledoves (Luke 2:24), which was what the law prescribed for people too poor to afford a lamb (Lev. 12:8). On that day, the little family from Nazareth encountered two elderly saints, Simeon and Anna. (Anna will be the subject of the following chapter.)

Simeon was an old man whom Scripture describes as "just and devout, waiting for the Consolation of Israel" (Luke 2:25 NKJV). The Spirit of God had revealed to Simeon that he would have the privilege of seeing the Messiah before he died. On the day Joseph and Mary dedicated Jesus at the temple, the Holy Spirit led Simeon there also (v. 27 NKJV).

As soon as Simeon saw Jesus, he knew this child was the Lord's Anointed One. Scripture says he took the infant Jesus up in his arms and uttered a prophecy. Then, turning to Mary, he told her, "Behold, this Child is destined for the fall and rising of many in Israel, and for a sign which will be spoken against (yes, *a sword will pierce through your own soul also),* that the thoughts of many hearts may be revealed" (vv. 34–35 NKJV, emphasis added).

It is almost certain that in the process of writing his gospel, Luke sought details about Jesus' birth and life from Mary. Luke 1:1–4 indicates that he had access to the testimony of many eyewitness reports. Since he included several details that only Mary could have known, we can be fairly sure that Mary herself was one of Luke's primary sources. Luke's inclusion of several facts from Jesus' early life (2:19, 48, 51) suggests that this was the case. Mary's own eyewitness testimony must also have been Luke's source for the account of Simeon's prophecy, for who but she could have known and recalled that incident? Apparently, the old man's cryptic prophecy had never left her mind.

Years later, as Mary stood watching a soldier thrust a sword into Jesus' side, she must have truly felt as if a sword had pierced her own soul also. At that very moment, she might well have recalled Simeon's prophecy, and suddenly its true meaning came home to her with full force.

While Mary quietly watched her Son die, others were screaming wicked taunts and insults at Him. Her sense of the injustice being done to Him must have been profound. After all, no one understood Jesus' absolute, sinless perfection better than Mary did. She had nurtured Him as an infant and brought Him up through childhood. No one could have loved Him more than she did. All those facts merely compounded the acute grief any mother would feel at such a horrible sight. The pain of Mary's anguish is almost unimaginable. Yet she stood, stoically, silently, when lesser women would have fled in horror, shrieked and thrashed around in panic, or simply collapsed in a heap from the overwhelming distress. Mary was clearly a woman of dignified grace and courage.

Mary seemed to understand that her steadfast presence at Jesus' side was the only kind of support she could give Him at this dreaded moment. But even that was merely a public show of support. Mary's personal suffering did not represent any kind of participation in His atoning work. Her grief added no merit to His suffering for others' guilt. *He* was bearing the sins of the world. She could not assist with that. Nor did He need her aid as any kind of "co-redemptrix" or "co-mediatrix." "There is one God and one Mediator between God and men, the Man Christ Jesus" (1 Tim. 2:5 NKJV). Mary herself did not try to intrude into that office; it is a shame so many people insist on trying to put her there.

As a matter of fact, in the waning hours of Jesus' life, it was *Jesus* who came to *her* aid. Already in the final throes of death, He spotted Mary standing nearby with a small group of women and John, the beloved disciple. For the final time, Jesus acknowledged His human relationship with Mary. In his own gospel account, John describes what happened: "When Jesus therefore saw His mother, and the disciple whom He loved standing by, He said to His mother, 'Woman, behold your son!' Then He said to the disciple, 'Behold your mother!' And from that hour that disciple took her to his own home" (John 19:26–27 NKJV).

So one of Jesus' last earthly acts before yielding up His life to God was to make sure that for the rest of her life, Mary would be cared for.

That act epitomizes Mary's relationship with her firstborn Son. She was His earthly mother; but He was her eternal Lord. She understood and embraced that relationship. She bowed to His authority in heavenly matters just as in His childhood and youth He had always been subject to her parental authority in earthly matters (Luke 2:51). As a mother, she had once provided all His needs, but in the ultimate and eternal sense, He was *her* Savior and provider.

Mary was like no other mother. Godly mothers are typically absorbed in the task of training their children for heaven. Mary's Son was the Lord and Creator of heaven. Over time, she came to perceive the full import of that truth, until it filled her heart. She became a disciple and a worshiper. Her maternal relationship with Him faded into the background. That moment on the cross—Jesus placing His mother into the earthly care of John—formally marked the end of that earthly aspect of Mary's relationship with Jesus.

After Jesus' death, Mary appears only once more in the Bible. In Luke's chronicle of the early church, she is listed among the disciples who were praying together in Jerusalem at Pentecost (Acts 1:14). Her name is never mentioned in the epistles. It is clear that the early church never thought of making her an object of religious veneration the way so many have done in the subsequent annals of various Christian traditions.

Mary herself never claimed to be, or pretended to be, anything more than a humble handmaiden of the Lord. She was extraordinary because

God used her in an extraordinary way. She clearly thought of herself as perfectly *ordinary*. She is portrayed in Scripture only as an instrument whom God used in the fulfillment of His plan. She herself never made any pretense of being an administrator of the divine agenda, and she never gave anyone any encouragement to regard her as a mediatrix in the dispensing of divine grace. The lowly perspective reflected in Mary's Magnificat is the same simple spirit of humility that colored all her life and character.

It is truly regrettable that religious superstition has, in effect, turned Mary into an idol. She is certainly a worthy woman to emulate, but Mary herself would undoubtedly be appalled to think anyone would pray to her, venerate images of her, or burn candles in homage to her. Her life and her testimony point us consistently to her Son. *He* was the object of her worship. *He* was the one she recognized as Lord. *He* was the one she trusted for everything. Mary's own example, seen in the pure light of Scripture, teaches us to do the same.

7

ANNA: THE FAITHFUL WITNESS

*She gave thanks to the Lord, and spoke of Him to all those who
looked for redemption in Jerusalem.*

Luke 2:38 NKJV

I t is truly remarkable that when Jesus was born, so few people in Israel
recognized their Messiah. It was not as if no one was watching for Him.
Messianic expectation in the early first century was running at an all-
time high.

Daniel's famous prophecy about "Messiah the Prince" (Dan. 9:24–27
NKJV) had practically set the date. Daniel wrote, "Seventy weeks are determined . . . Know therefore and understand, that from the going forth of
the command to restore and build Jerusalem until Messiah the Prince, there
shall be seven weeks and sixty-two weeks." If Daniel's "weeks" (literally,
"sevens" in the Hebrew) are understood as seven-year periods, Daniel is
describing a period of 483 years total: "seven weeks" (forty-nine years) plus
"sixty-two weeks" (434 years). "The command to restore and build
Jerusalem" seems to be a reference to the decree of Artaxerxes (Neh. 2:1–8),
which was issued in 444 or 445 BC. If the years are reckoned by a lunar
calendar of 360 days, Daniel's timetable would put the appearance of

"Messiah the Prince" around AD 30, which was the year of His triumphal entry.

Scripture records that when John the Baptist began his ministry, "The people were in expectation, and all reasoned in their hearts about John, whether he was the Christ or not" (Luke 3:15 NKJV). As a matter of fact, several of the disciples first encountered Christ for the very reason that they were watching expectantly for Him to appear, and they came to John the Baptist, who pointed the way to Christ (John 1:27–37).

The fact is, virtually all faithful believers in Israel were already expectantly awaiting the Messiah and looking diligently for Him at the exact time Jesus was born. The irony is that so very few recognized Him, because He met none of their expectations. They were looking for a mighty political and military leader who would become a conquering king; He was born into a peasant family. They probably anticipated that He would arrive with great fanfare and pageantry; He was born in a stable, almost in secret.

The only people in Israel who *did* recognize Christ at His birth were humble, unremarkable people. The Magi of Matthew 2:1–12, of course, were foreigners and Gentiles, and they were very rich, powerful, and influential men in their own culture. But the only *Israelites* who understood that Jesus was the Messiah at His birth were Mary and Joseph, the shepherds, Simeon, and Anna. All of them were basically nobodies. All of them recognized Him because they were told who He was by angels, or by some other form of special revelation. Luke recounts all their stories in succession, as if he is calling multiple witnesses, one at a time, to establish the matter. The final witness he calls is Anna. Everything Scripture has to say about her is contained in just three verses: Luke 2: 36–38. She is never mentioned anywhere else in the Bible. But these three verses are enough to establish her reputation as a genuinely extraordinary woman:

> *Now there was one, Anna, a prophetess, the daughter of Phanuel, of the tribe*
> *of Asher. She was of a great age, and had lived with a husband seven years*

from her virginity; and this woman was a widow of about eighty-four years,
who did not depart from the temple, but served God with fastings and
prayers night and day. And coming in that instant she gave thanks to the
Lord, and spoke of Him to all those who looked for redemption in Jerusalem.
(NKJV)

The scene is the same one we left near the end of our previous chapter. Simeon had just picked up the infant Jesus and pronounced a prophetic blessing on Him. "In that instant," Luke says, Anna happened by and immediately understood what was going on and who Christ was. Perhaps she overheard Simeon's blessing. She probably already knew Simeon personally. Anna herself was clearly a fixture in the temple, and Simeon was described as "just and devout" (v. 25 NKJV). Both were very old. It seems unlikely that their paths had never crossed. Probably knowing Simeon's reputation as a righteous man whose one expectation in life was to see "the Consolation of Israel" with his own eyes before dying, Anna stopped and took notice when she heard the joyous blessing he pronounced on Jesus.

Like every other extraordinary woman we have seen so far, Anna's hopes and dreams were full of messianic expectation. She knew the Old Testament promises, and she understood that salvation from sin and the future blessing of Israel depended on the coming of the Messiah. Her longing to see Him was suddenly and surprisingly fulfilled one day as she went about her normal routine in the temple.

Anna appears only in a very brief vignette of Luke's gospel, but her inclusion there elevates the importance of her life and testimony. She was blessed by God to be one of a handful of key witnesses who knew and understood the significance of Jesus' birth. And she made no attempt to keep it a secret. Thus she became one of the first and most enduring witnesses to Christ. No doubt wherever Luke's gospel is proclaimed, her testimony is still bringing others to the Savior. Thus she deserves a prominent place in any list of extraordinary women.

Actually, quite a lot about Anna's extraordinary life can be gleaned from the three brief verses of Scripture that are devoted to her story. Luke's narrative is loaded with key phrases that give us a surprisingly rich understanding of Anna's life and character.

"SHE WAS A PROPHETESS"

Luke introduced her this way: "There was one, Anna, a prophetess" (Luke 2:36 NKJV). Her name in Hebrew is identical to "Hannah." Remember, from the story of Samuel's mother Hannah, the name means "grace"—an appropriate name for a godly, dignified woman. Anna's character does bear some striking similarities to her Old Testament namesake. Both women were singled out for their practice of prayer and fasting. Both were perfectly at home in the temple. Both prophesied. In Hannah's case, you'll recall, her celebratory prayer (1 Sam. 2:1–10) was also a prophetic psalm about the Messiah. Anna is said to be a prophetess whose heart was prepared for the coming of the Messiah.

What did Luke mean by *prophetess*? He was not suggesting that Anna predicted the future. She was not a fortune-teller. He didn't necessarily even suggest that she received special revelation from God. The word *prophetess* simply designated a woman who spoke the Word of God. Any preacher who faithfully proclaims the Word of God would be a "prophet" in the general biblical sense. And a prophetess would be a woman uniquely devoted to declaring the Word of God.

Anna may have been a teacher of the Old Testament to other women. Or she may have simply had a private ministry there in the temple offering words of encouragement and instruction from the Hebrew Scriptures to other women who came to worship. Nothing suggests that she was a source of revelation, or that any special revelation ever came to her directly. Even her realization that Jesus was the Messiah seemed to have come from the revelation given to Simeon and subsequently overheard by her. She is nonetheless called a prophetess because it was her habit to declare the truth of God's Word to others. This gift for proclaiming God's truth ultimately played a major role in the ministry she is still best remembered for.

In all the Old Testament, only five women are ever referred to as "prophetess." The first was Miriam, Moses' sister, identified as a prophetess in Exodus 15:20, where she led the women of Israel in a psalm of praise to God about the drowning of Pharaoh and his army. The simple one-stanza psalm Miriam sang was the substance of her only recorded prophecy (v. 21). The fact that God had once spoken through her, unfortunately, later became an occasion for pride and rebellion (Num. 12:1–2), and the Lord disciplined her for that sin by temporarily smiting her with leprosy (vv. 9–15).

Miriam / pride

In Judges 4:4, we are introduced to the second woman in the Old Testament designated as a prophetess: "Deborah, a prophetess, the wife of Lapidoth" (Judg. 4:4 NKJV). She was the only female among the varied assortment of judges who led the Jewish people before the monarchy was established in Israel. In fact, she was the only woman in all of Scripture who ever held that kind of leadership position and was blessed for it. The Lord seemed to raise her up as a rebuke to the men of her generation who were paralyzed by fear. She saw herself not as a usurper of men, but as a woman who functioned in a maternal capacity, while men like Barak were being raised up to step into their proper roles of leadership (5:12). That's why she referred to herself as "a mother in Israel" (v. 7 NKJV). She gave instructions to Barak from the Lord (Judg. 4:6), so it seems she received revelation from God, at least on that one occasion.

Deborah / judge

In 2 Kings 22:14, Scripture mentions Huldah as a prophetess. In verses 15–20, she had a word from the Lord for Hilkiah the priest and others. Nothing about her, or her background, is known. In fact, she is mentioned only here and in a parallel passage in 2 Chronicles 34:22–28.

Huldah

The only two other women called prophetesses in the Old Testament

Noadiah

were an otherwise unknown woman named Noadiah (Neh. 6:14), who was classified among the *false* prophets; and Isaiah's wife (Isa. 8:3), who was called a prophetess only because she was married to Isaiah, not because she herself prophesied (unless her decision to name her son "Maher-Shalal-Hash-Baz" could be counted as a prophecy).

Rarely did God speak to his people through women, and never did any woman have an ongoing prophetic ministry similar to that of Elijah, Isaiah, or any of the other key Old Testament prophets. In other words, there is nothing anywhere in Scripture to indicate that any women ever held a prophetic *office*. The idea that "prophetess" was a technical term for an official position or an ongoing ministry of direct revelation is simply nowhere to be found in Scripture.

Luke's identification of Anna as a "prophetess," therefore, did not necessarily mean that she personally received divine revelation. When Luke called her a "prophetess," we are not to imagine that this was an *office* she filled. Most likely, it meant that she had a reputation as a gifted teacher of other women and a faithful encourager of her fellow worshipers in the temple. When she spoke, it was about the Word of God. She had evidently spent a lifetime hiding God's Word in her heart. Naturally, that was the substance of what she usually had to say. So when Luke called her a "prophetess," he gave insight into her character and a clue about what occupied her mind and her conversation.

"OF THE TRIBE OF ASHER"

Anna is further identified as "the daughter of Phanuel, of the tribe of Asher" (Luke 2:36 NKJV). Her heritage is given because it was rather unusual. Asher was the eighth son of Jacob. He was the offspring of Zilpah, Leah's maid and Jacob's concubine (Gen. 30:12–13). The tribe that descended from Asher belonged to the apostate northern kingdom of Israel.

If you remember Old Testament history, you know that the kingdom split after Solomon's time. The ten tribes in the north formed an independent nation, with their own king (who was not the rightful heir to David's throne, but a usurper). From then on, in the Old Testament, the name "Israel" applied to the apostate northern kingdom. The southern kingdom took the name "Judah." (That was because Judah was by far the larger of the two remaining tribes in the south—the other one being Benjamin.)

The southern kingdom remained loyal to the Davidic throne. Of course, the city of Jerusalem lay in the heart of the southern kingdom close to the border between Judah and Benjamin. The temple there was still the only place where the true priesthood could offer sacrifices. A few faithful Israelites from each of the ten tribes migrated south so that they weren't cut off from the temple, but in doing so, they gave up their family lands and their inheritance.

Judah and Israel remained independent from one another for generations. At times they were uneasy allies. Most of the time, however, their kings were bitter rivals. Apostasy and idolatry plagued both nations continually. Prophets were sent by God to warn the northern as well as the southern tribes about their spiritual decline, but the prophets were mostly spurned on both sides of the border. Evil kings sat on both thrones. Judah had a few good and godly kings in the mix, but every one of the kings of Israel was evil.

Naturally, apostate Israel built new places of worship and established an alternative priesthood. That quickly led to the total corruption of the Jewish religion in the northern kingdom. Ever more sinister forms of paganism saturated the culture. Finally, in 722 BC, the Assyrians conquered the ten northern tribes and took most of the people into captivity. Only a handful ever returned.

722 BC

Anna's descent from the tribe of Asher suggests that her heritage owed much to God's grace. Her ancestors had either migrated south before the Assyrian conquest of Israel, or they were among the small and scattered group of exiles who returned from captivity. Either way, she was part of the believing remnant from the northern kingdom, and she was therefore a living emblem of God's faithfulness to His people.

"THIS WOMAN WAS A WIDOW"

By the time of Jesus' birth, Anna was already advanced in years. She had not enjoyed a particularly easy life. Her whole world was shattered by tragedy when she was still quite young, apparently before she had even borne children. Her husband died seven years after their marriage, and she had remained single ever since.

The Greek text is ambiguous as to her exact age. ("This woman was a widow of about eighty-four years.") It might mean literally that she had been a widow for eighty-four years. Assuming she married very young (remember, thirteen was a typical age for engagement in that society), then lived with her husband seven years before he died, that would make her at least 104—very old indeed, but entirely possible.

More likely, what the text is saying is that she was now an eighty-four-year-old widow. She was married for seven years when her husband died, and having never remarried, she had now lived as a widow for more than six decades.

Widowhood in that society was extremely difficult. It virtually guaranteed a life of extreme poverty. That's why, in the early church, the apostle Paul urged young widows to remarry (1 Tim. 5:14) so that the church was not overly burdened with their support.

Anna probably either lived on charity or supported herself out of the remnants of her family's inheritance. Either way, she must have led a very frugal, chaste, and sober life. Luke adds that she "served God with fastings and prayers night and day" (Luke 2:37 NKJV)—which rounds out the picture of this elderly, dignified, quiet, devoted woman's life and ministry.

"WHO DID NOT DEPART FROM THE TEMPLE"

Luke gave another significant detail about Anna: "[She] did not depart from the temple" (Luke 2:37 NKJV). That's an emphatic statement, which suggests that Luke meant it in a literal sense. Evidently, Anna lived right there on the temple grounds. There were some apartments in the outer courts (Neh. 13:7–9). These were modest chambers, probably used as temporary dwelling places for priests who lived on the temple grounds while doing their two weeks' annual service.

Perhaps because of her long faithfulness, her obvious spiritual gifts, her steadfast devotion to the Lord, and her constant commitment to her ministry of prayer and fasting, temple officials had given her a small chamber. She was now too old to be employed as a caretaker, but perhaps she had once served in that capacity, and her living quarters had been given to her for life. In any case, it was ultimately the Lord who had graciously provided her a place in His house and sovereignly orchestrated whatever arrangement she might have had with the temple custodians.

It is obvious that Anna was a most extraordinary woman in the eyes of everyone who knew her. She lived the simplest kind of life. She could *always* be found at the temple. She was singularly and completely devoted to the service and worship of God—mostly through her prayers and fasting.

The manner of her praying, accompanied by fasting, speaks of her own self-denial and sincerity. Fasting by itself is not a particularly useful exercise. Abstaining from food *per se* has no mystical effect on anything spiritual. But fasting *with prayer* reveals a heart so consumed with praying, and so eager to receive the blessing being sought, that the person simply has no interest in eating. That is when fasting has real value.

Anna apparently had been doing this as a pattern for sixty-four years or longer. Here was a passionate woman! What do you think Anna had been praying about? She surely prayed about many things, but there is little doubt that one of the main subjects of her prayers was an earnest plea for the very same thing Simeon was so eager for: "the Consolation of Israel" (Luke 2:25 NKJV). Her hope, like Eve's, was for the Seed who would crush the serpent's head. Her longing, like Sarah's, was for the Seed of Abraham, who would bless all the nations of the world. She was praying that God would soon send the promised deliverer, the Messiah.

Anna's amazing faith stemmed from the fact that she believed all the promises that filled the Old Testament. She took the Word of God seriously. She knew in her heart that the Messiah was coming, and without any doubt whatsoever her first and foremost prayer was that it would happen soon.

I'm convinced that Anna had a remarkable knowledge of spiritual truth. Remember, she belonged to the believing remnant, not the apostate majority. She had no part in the error and hypocrisy that Jesus would later rebuke among the scribes and Pharisees. She was not a participant in the money-changing system at the temple that stirred His wrath. She knew the Pharisees were corrupt legalists. She understood that the Sadducees were spiritually bankrupt liberals. She truly loved her God. She understood His heart and mind. She genuinely believed His Word. She was a wonderfully remarkable woman indeed—perhaps one of the *most* devout people we meet anywhere on the pages of Scripture. No one else comes to mind who fasted and prayed faithfully for more than sixty years!

God was about to give her an answer to her prayers in the most dramatic fashion. Verse 38 says that just when Simeon pronounced his prophetic blessing on the infant Christ and His earthly parents, "in that instant" (NKJV), she came along. Now, Herod's temple was a massive building, and the temple complex was huge, surrounded by a courtyard with thousands of people milling around at almost any given time.

Joseph and Mary did not know Simeon, but by God's providence and through the sovereign direction of His Spirit, He had brought them together (v. 27). At that very instant, just while Simeon was blessing the child with inspired words of prophecy, the Spirit of God providentially led this elderly woman to a place where she was within earshot. Luke's description is typically understated: "Coming in that instant she gave thanks to the Lord" (v. 38 NKJV).

Suddenly everything she had been praying and fasting for was right there in front of her face, wrapped in a little bundle in Simeon's arms. By faith, she knew instantly that Simeon's prophecy was true and that God had answered her prayers. She immediately began giving thanks to God, and all those many, many years of petition turned to praise.

We can only imagine how Anna felt after long decades of focused prayer and fasting, yearning for God to reveal His glory again, praying and fasting for the salvation of Israel, and beseeching God to send the Messiah. Finally, the answer to her prayers had come in flesh and blood.

"SHE . . . SPOKE OF HIM TO ALL"

Suddenly Anna's prophetic giftedness came boldly to the forefront: "[She] spoke of Him to all those who looked for redemption in Jerusalem" (Luke 2:38 NKJV). The verb tense signifies continuous action. It literally means that she continually spoke of Him to all who were looking for the Redeemer. This became her one message for the rest of her life.

Notice that Anna knew who the believing remnant were. She could identify the *true* worshipers—the ones who, like her, were expectantly awaiting the Messiah. She sought such people out, and at every opportunity from then on, she spoke to them about *Him*.

That is how this dear woman who had spent so many years mostly talking to God became best known for talking to people about Christ. The Messiah had finally come, and Anna was one of the very first to know who He was. She could not keep that news to herself. She thus became one of the very first and most enduring witnesses of Christ.

What became of Anna after this is not recorded. She was undoubtedly in heaven by the time Christ began his public ministry some thirty years later. The day of His dedication was probably her one and only glimpse of Him. But it was enough for her. She literally could not stop talking about Him.

And that is the most endearing part of this wonderful woman's extraordinary legacy.

8

THE SAMARITAN WOMAN: FINDING THE WATER OF LIFE

Come, see a Man who told me all things that I ever did. Could this be the Christ?

John 4:29 NKJV

I n John 4 we meet an unnamed Samaritan woman with a rather sordid background. Jesus met her when she came to draw water at a well, and the encounter transformed her whole life. The apostle John devoted forty-two verses to telling the tale of this woman's amazing encounter with the Lord. Such a significant section of Scripture would not be given to this one episode unless the lessons it contained were supremely important.

At first glance, much about the scene seems ordinary and unimportant. Here is an anonymous woman who performed the most mundane of everyday tasks: she came to draw her daily ration of water for her household. She came alone, at an hour when she probably expected to find no one else at the well. (That was probably an indication of her status as an outcast.) Jesus, traveling through the region on His way to Jerusalem, was resting near the well. His disciples were purchasing food in the nearby village. Jesus, having no utensil or rope with which to draw water, asked the woman to fetch Him a drink. It was not the stuff of great drama, and this was certainly not a scene that would lead us to expect one of the most profound theological lessons in all the Bible was just ahead.

A REMARKABLE SETTING

Look closer, however, and it turns out that many details in this picture are enormously significant.

In the first place, this was Jacob's well, located on a plot of land well known to students of the Old Testament. It was a field that Jacob purchased so that he could pitch his tent in the land of Canaan (Gen. 33:18–19). He built an altar on the site, "and called it El Elohe Israel," meaning "the God of Israel" (v. 20 NKJV). This very field was the first inhabitable piece of real estate recorded in Scripture that any Israelite ever owned in the Promised Land. Abraham had previously purchased the field of Ephron, which contained a cave that became his and Sarah's burial place (Gen. 23:17–18; 25:9–10). But *this* property actually became Jacob's home base.

John 4:5 reminds us that this was the same parcel of ground Jacob deeded to his favorite son, Joseph (Gen. 48:21–22). It later became the very place where Joseph's bones were finally put to rest (Josh. 24:32). Remember that when Moses left Egypt, he took Joseph's coffin (Gen. 50:24–26; Ex. 13:19). The Israelites carried Joseph's remains around with them for forty years in the wilderness. One of their first acts after conquering the Promised Land was the final interment of those bones. This was all done at Joseph's own behest (Heb. 11:22). To the Israelites, the tale of Joseph's bones was a significant reminder of God's faithfulness (Acts 7:15–16).

The well that was on the property was not mentioned in the Old Testament, but its location was well established in Jesus' day by centuries of Jewish tradition, and the site remains a major landmark even today. The well is very deep (John 4:11), accessible only by a very long rope through a hole dug though a slab of soft limestone. The reservoir below is spring-fed, so its water is always fresh, pure, and cold. It is the *only* well, and the finest water, in a vicinity where brackish springs abound. The existence of such a well on Jacob's property was deemed by the Israelites as a token of God's grace and goodness to their patriarch. Hence, the location had a very long and meaningful history in Jewish tradition.

In Jesus' era, though, that plot of ground lay in Samaritan territory, and this is another surprising and significant detail about the setting in John 4. For Jesus to be in Samaria at all was unusual (and perhaps even somewhat scandalous). The Samaritans were considered unclean by the Israelites. Jesus was traveling from Jerusalem to Galilee (v. 3). A look at any map reveals that the most direct route goes straight through Samaria. But in Jesus' time, any self-respecting Jew would always travel a different way. The preferred route went east of the Jordan River, then north through Decapolis before crossing the Jordan again into Galilee. This alternate route went many miles out of the way, but it bypassed Samaria, and that was the whole point.

Samaritans were a mixed-race people descended from pagans who had intermarried with the few remaining Israelites after the Assyrians conquered the northern kingdom (722 BC). As early as Nehemiah's time (the mid-fifth century BC), the Samaritans posed a serious threat to the purity of Israel. Secular history records that Nehemiah's main nemesis, Sanballat, was an early governor of Samaria (Neh. 4:1–2). The Jewish high priest's grandson married Sanballat's daughter, incurring Nehemiah's wrath. "I drove him from me," Nehemiah wrote (13:28 NKJV). Such a marriage "defiled the priesthood and the covenant of the priesthood and the Levites" (v. 29 NKJV).

By the first century, the Samaritans had a distinct culture built around a syncretistic religion, blending aspects of Judaism and rank paganism. Their place of worship was on Mount Gerizim. Sanballat had built a temple there to rival the temple in Jerusalem. The Samaritan temple was served by a false priesthood, of course. Remember that the Israelites in the northern kingdom had already corrupted Judaism several centuries before this by establishing a false priesthood. That defiled flavor of Judaism was precisely what gave birth to Samaritanism. So the Samaritan religion was twice removed from the truth. But they did hold to selected elements of Jewish doctrine. Samaritans regarded the Pentateuch (the first five books of the Old Testament) as Scripture. They rejected the psalms and the prophets, however.

During the Maccabean period, less than a century and a half before the time of Christ, Jewish armies under John Hyrcanus destroyed the Samaritan temple. Gerizim nevertheless remained sacred to the Samaritans and the center of worship for their religion. (A group of Samaritans still worships there even today.)

The Jews' contempt for the Samaritans was so intense by the first century that most Jews simply refused to travel through Samaria, despite the importance of that land to their heritage.

Jesus deliberately broke with convention. John 4:4 says, "He *needed* to go through Samaria" (NKJV, emphasis added). He had a purpose to fulfill, and it required Him to travel through Samaria, stop at this historic well, talk to this troubled woman, and make an unprecedented disclosure of His true mission and identity.

Seen in that light, virtually *everything* about the setting of John 4 becomes remarkable. It is unusual to find Jesus alone. It is amazing to realize that God incarnate could grow physically weary (v. 6) or become thirsty (v. 7). It is startling that Jesus would intentionally seek out and initiate a conversation with a wretched Samaritan woman like this one. It was astonishing even to *her* that any Jewish man would speak to her (v. 9). It was equally shocking for the disciples to find Him speaking to her (v. 27). It would have been considered outrageous for Him to drink from an unclean vessel that belonged to an unclean woman. It seems odd for a woman like this to enter so quickly into an extended theological dialogue. It is marvelous to see how rich Jesus' teaching could be, even in a context like this. (The heart and soul of everything Scripture teaches about authentic worship is condensed in just a few words Jesus spoke to this woman in verses 21–24.) It is astounding that her own sin was such a large issue in her own heart and mind (v. 29), even though Jesus had only referred to it obliquely (v. 18) and even though she initially seemed to try to dodge the point (vv. 19–20).

But what is staggeringly unexpected about this whole fantastic account is that Jesus chose *this* time and *this* place and *this* woman to be part of the setting where He would (for the first time ever) formally and explicitly unveil His true identity as the Messiah.

And that singular fact automatically gives this woman a prominent place in the "extraordinary" category.

A CURIOUS CONVERSATION

Jesus' conversation with the woman started out simply and naturally enough—he asked her for a drink. The well was deep, and He had no way to draw water from it, so He said: "Give Me a drink" (v. 7 NKJV). He probably said it casually and in a friendly enough way, but He expressed it in the form of a command, not a question.

She obviously didn't think the request, or the way He phrased it, was rude. She certainly didn't act offended. Instead, she immediately expressed surprise that He would even speak to her, much less drink from her vessel: "How is it that You, being a Jew, ask a drink from me, a Samaritan woman?" (v. 9 NKJV). Gender taboos, racial divisions, and the class system would normally keep a man of Jesus' status from conversing with a woman such as she, much less drinking from a water container that belonged to her.

Bypassing her actual question, Jesus said, "If you knew the gift of God, and who it is who says to you, 'Give Me a drink,' you would have asked

Him, and He would have given you living water" (v. 10 NKJV). He was already hinting at the real message He intended to give her.

She immediately understood that He was making an amazing claim. She replied, "Sir, You have nothing to draw with, and the well is deep. Where then do You get that living water? Are You greater than our father Jacob, who gave us the well, and drank from it himself, as well as his sons and his livestock?" (vv. 11–12 NKJV).

As a matter of fact, He *was* greater than Jacob, and that is precisely the point He wanted to demonstrate for her. But once more, instead of answering her question directly, He continued speaking of the living water. Indeed, He assured her, the water He offered was infinitely better than the water from Jacob's well: "Whoever drinks of this water will thirst again, but whoever drinks of the water that I shall give him will never thirst. But the water that I shall give him will become in him a fountain of water springing up into everlasting life" (vv. 13–14 NKJV).

Now she was supremely curious, and she asked Him to give her the living water (v. 15). I think by now she probably understood that He was speaking of spiritual water. Parables and metaphors were standard teaching tools in that culture. Jesus was obviously some kind of rabbi or spiritual leader. It is unlikely that she was still thinking in literal terms. But her reply simply echoed the same metaphorical language He had used with her: "Sir, give me this water, that I may not thirst, nor come here to draw" (v. 15 NKJV).

Jesus' next words unexpectedly drew her up short: "Go, call your husband, and come here" (v. 16 NKJV).

Now she was in a quandary. The truth about her life was so horrible that she could not admit it to Him. He seemed to be assuming she was a typical woman with a respectable home and an honorable husband. She was nothing like that. But instead of exposing all her disgrace to this rabbi, she told him only a small fraction of the truth: "I have no husband" (v. 17 NKJV).

To her utter chagrin, He knew the full truth already: "Jesus said to her, 'You have well said, 'I have no husband,' for you have had five husbands, and the one whom you now have is not your husband; in that you spoke truly'" (vv. 17–18 NKJV). Notice that He did not rebuke her as a liar; on the contrary, He *commended* her for speaking truthfully. She wasn't denying her sin. But she obviously wasn't proud of it, either. So in order to retain whatever shred of dignity she could, she had simply sidestepped the implications of His question without actually lying to cover anything up.

No matter. He knew all about her sin right down to the infinitesimal details. When she later recounted her meeting with Jesus, this was the fact that left the strongest impression on her mind: He told her everything she ever did (vv. 29, 39). Moments before, she had questioned whether He was greater than Jacob. Now she knew.

I love the low-key, almost droll simplicity with which she acknowledged her own guilt: "Sir, I perceive that You are a prophet" (v. 19 NKJV). He had unmasked her completely. Whoever He was, He obviously knew all about her. And yet, far from spurning her or castigating her, He had offered her the water of life!

At this point, a thousand thoughts and questions must have filled her mind. She certainly must have wondered exactly who this was and how He knew so much about her. It is obvious that He was quite prepared to tell her who He was. He Himself had raised that issue almost immediately (v. 10). But instead of pursuing that question, she turned the conversation in a bizarre direction. She brought up what was to her mind the biggest point of religious contention between the Jews and the Samaritans: "Our fathers worshiped on this mountain, and you Jews say that in Jerusalem is the place where one ought to worship" (v. 20 NKJV). She actually didn't frame it as a question, but I don't think she meant it as a challenge. I think she was genuinely hoping that this rabbi, who seemed to know *everything*, could straighten out what seemed to her to be the fundamental debate of the ages: Who was right? The Jews or the Samaritans? Gerizim or Jerusalem?

Jesus did not brush her sincere question aside. He didn't reproach her for changing the subject. He gave her a brief but very potent answer in John 4:21–24:

Woman, believe Me, the hour is coming when you will neither on this mountain, nor in Jerusalem, worship the Father. You worship what you do not know; we know what we worship, for salvation is of the Jews. But the hour is coming, and now is, when the true worshipers will worship the Father in spirit and truth; for the Father is seeking such to worship Him. God is Spirit, and those who worship Him must worship in spirit and truth. (NKJV)

With that reply, He accomplished several things. First, he let her know that *where* you worship isn't the issue. True worshipers are defined by whom and how they worship.

Second, He made it clear that the religious tradition she had grown up in was totally and utterly false: "You worship what you do not know; we know what we worship, for salvation is of the Jews" (v. 22 NKJV). He did not airbrush the reality or trouble Himself with trying to be delicate. He answered the real question she was asking.

Third, He subtly steered her back to the main subject by telling her that a new age was dawning when neither Gerizim nor Jerusalem would have a monopoly on the priesthood. The era of the New Covenant was just on the horizon. There was a subtle expression of messianic expectation in His words, and she got it.

She replied with these amazing words: "'I know that Messiah is coming' (who is called Christ). 'When He comes, He will tell us all things'" (v. 25 NKJV).

Is it not significant that this Samaritan woman, born and raised in a culture of corrupt religion, had the same messianic hope shared by every other godly woman in Scripture?

Now, consider the implications of her statement. She *knew* the Messiah was coming. That was a definitive expression of confidence. It was embryonic faith waiting to be born. And how did she think the true Messiah would identify Himself? "When He comes, He will tell us all things" (v. 25 NKJV). Jesus had already demonstrated His full knowledge of all her secrets. As she later testified to the men of her city, "[He] told me all things that I ever did" (v. 29 NKJV).

She was strongly hinting that she suspected Jesus Himself might be the Messiah. When the apostle Peter later confessed his faith that Jesus *was* the Christ, the Son of the living God, Jesus told him, "Blessed are you, Simon Bar-Jonah, for flesh and blood has not revealed this to you, but My Father who is in heaven" (Matt. 16:17 NKJV). The same thing was true of this woman. The Holy Spirit was working in her heart. God the Father was drawing her irresistibly to Christ, revealing truth to her that eye had never seen and ear had never heard.

Now Jesus was ready to pull back the curtain and reveal His true identity in an unprecedented way.

AN ASTONISHING REVELATION

No sooner had she broached the subject of the Messiah, than Jesus said, "I who speak to you am He" (John 4:26 NKJV). This is the single most direct and explicit messianic claim Jesus ever made. Never before in any of the biblical record had He said this so forthrightly to anyone. Never again is it recorded that He declared Himself this plainly, until the night of His betrayal.

Of course, when Peter made his great confession, Jesus affirmed that Peter had it right (Matt. 16:17–19). But He immediately "commanded His disciples that they should tell no one that He was Jesus the Christ" (v. 20 NKJV). When Jewish crowds demanded, "If You are the Christ, tell us plainly" (John 10:24 NKJV), He never denied the truth, but He avoided explicitly stating the words they were clamoring to hear. Instead, He appealed to His works as evidence of who He was: "I told you, and you do not believe. The works that I do in My Father's name, they bear witness of Me" (v. 25 NKJV).

It was not until His trial before Caiaphas, in the early-morning hours just before His crucifixion, that Jesus once again revealed His identity as plainly as He did for this Samaritan woman.

The high priest asked Him, "Are You the Christ, the Son of the Blessed?" (Mark 14:61 NKJV).

Jesus said, "I am. And you will see the Son of Man sitting at the right hand of the Power, and coming with the clouds of heaven" (v. 62 NKJV).

That was the very declaration that ultimately cost Him His life. Mark wrote, "The high priest tore his clothes and said, 'What further need do we have of witnesses? You have heard the blasphemy! What do you think?' And they all condemned Him to be deserving of death" (vv. 63–64 NKJV).

In light of all that, it is absolutely astonishing that the very *first* time Jesus chose to reveal Himself as Messiah, it was to a Samaritan woman with such a shady past. But His self-revelation is a testimony to her faith. The fact that He declared Himself so plainly is proof positive that the tiny germ of hope that had her looking for the Messiah in the first place was either about to develop into authentic, full-fledged faith—or else it already had sprouted. Jesus would not have committed Himself to an unbeliever (John 2:24).

Scripture says it was precisely "at this point" that the disciples returned from their errand, "and they marveled that He talked with a woman" (John 4:27 NKJV). The Greek expression is emphatic, suggesting they returned just in time to hear Him declare Himself Messiah. They were shocked speechless at the scene. John, himself an eyewitness, wrote, "No one said, 'What do You seek?' or, 'Why are You talking with her?'" (v. 27 NKJV).

AN AMAZING TRANSFORMATION

Soon after the disciples arrived, the woman left the well, leaving behind her water pot. It wasn't absent-mindedness that caused her to leave it; she fully intended to come back. Her plan was to bring the leading men of the city and introduce them to Christ. She was privy to amazing knowledge that must not be kept secret.

Her response was typical of new believers, one of the evidences of authentic faith. The person who has just had the burden of sin and guilt lifted always wants to share the good news with others. The woman's excitement would have been palpable. And notice that the first thing she told the men of her town was that Jesus had told her everything she ever did. No longer was she evading the facts of her sin. She was basking in the glow of forgiveness, and there is simply no shame in that.

Her enthusiasm and determination were apparently hard to resist, because the men of the city went back with her to the well where they all met Jesus.

The immediate impact of this woman's testimony on the city of Sychar was profound. John wrote, "Many of the Samaritans of that city believed in Him *because of the word of the woman* who testified, 'He told me all that I ever did'" (v. 39 NKJV, emphasis added).

What a contrast this makes with the reception Jesus got from the scribes and Pharisees in Jerusalem! Luke wrote, "The Pharisees and scribes *complained,* saying, 'This Man receives sinners and eats with them'" (Luke 15:2 NKJV, emphasis added). The religious leaders were disgusted with Him because He was willing to converse with rogues and scoundrels such as this woman. They mocked Him openly, saying, "Look, a glutton and a winebibber, a friend of tax collectors and sinners!" (Matt. 11:19 NKJV). They were offended, for example, when Jesus went to the house of

Zacchaeus. "They all complained, saying, 'He has gone to be a guest with a man who is a sinner'" (Luke 19:7 NKJV).

But Samaritans lacked the phony scruples of religious hypocrisy. The leading men of that Samaritan village were in many ways the polar opposites of the religious leaders in Jerusalem. The Jewish leaders, of course, were convinced that when the Messiah came, He would vindicate them. He would banish the Romans and set up His kingdom over the whole world, with Israel at the hub. He would triumph over all Israel's enemies, including the Samaritans, and rule and reign through the very political and religious structures they represented. Their messianic expectations were high for that very reason, and their contempt for Christ was acute for the *same* reason. He fit none of their preconceived notions of what the Messiah ought to be. He rebuked the religious leaders while fellowshiping openly with publicans and sinners. The Jewish leaders hated Him for it.

The Samaritans had the opposite perspective. They knew the Messiah was promised. Although the books of Moses were the only part of the Old Testament they believed, the messianic promises were there. As Jesus told the Pharisees, "If you believed Moses, you would believe Me; for he wrote about Me" (John 5:46 NKJV). In Deuteronomy 18:18, for example, God promised a great Prophet—a national spokesman on the order of Moses, or greater: "I will raise up for them a Prophet like you from among their brethren, and will put My words in His mouth" (NKJV). The Pentateuch also included all the familiar promises about the Seed of the woman who would crush the serpent, and the Seed of Abraham, in whom all the nations would be blessed. That is why the Samaritan woman knew the Messiah was coming.

But Samaritan society had been degraded and debased by years of false religion and immorality. Samaritans had a definite sense that they were sinners. They lacked the self-righteous swagger that colored the religion of the Pharisees and Sadducees. When they pondered the coming Messiah, they probably anticipated His advent with a degree of fear.

So when this woman announced so boldly that she had found the Messiah and that He knew everything about her sin but received her anyway, the men of Sychar welcomed Jesus with great enthusiasm. "They urged Him to stay with them; and He stayed there two days. And many more believed because of His own word. Then they said to the woman, 'Now we believe, not because of what you said, for we ourselves have heard Him and we know that this is indeed the Christ, the Savior of the world'" (John 4:40–42 NKJV). This was an amazing revival, and it must have utterly transformed that little town.

Jesus had indeed found a true worshiper. Scripture doesn't tell us what ultimately became of the Samaritan woman. Her *heart* was clearly changed by her encounter with Christ. It is an absolute certainty that her *life* changed as well, because "If anyone is in Christ, [she] is a new creation; old things have passed away; behold, all things have become new" (2 Cor. 5:17 NKJV).

Within three years after the Samaritan woman's meeting with Christ at Jacob's well, the church was founded. Its influence quickly spread from Jerusalem into all Judea and Samaria, and from there to the uttermost parts of the earth (Acts 1:8). That meant the Samaritan woman and the men of her city would soon be able to find fellowship and teaching in a context where there was neither Hebrew nor Samaritan, Jew nor Greek, slave nor free, male nor female; but where all were one in Christ Jesus (Gal. 3:28). I think it is a certainty that the Samaritan village of Sychar became a center of gospel activity and witness. Having gone out of His way to reveal Himself to that village, having given them the water of life that quenched their spiritual thirst, we can be certain He did not simply abandon them. This woman, who had begun her new life by bringing many others to Christ, no doubt continued her evangelistic ministry. She even continues it today through the record of Scripture. Multitudes have come to Christ through the influence of John 4 and "because of the word of the woman who testified, 'He told me all that I ever did'" (v. 39 NKJV). Only heaven will reveal the vast and far-reaching fruits of this extraordinary woman's encounter with the Messiah.

9

MARTHA AND MARY: WORKING AND WORSHIPING

❦

Mary . . . sat at Jesus' feet and heard His word. But Martha was distracted with much serving.

Luke 10:39–40 NKJV

I n this chapter, we meet *two* extraordinary women—Martha and Mary. We'll consider them together because that is how Scripture consistently presents them. They lived with their brother, Lazarus, in the small village of Bethany. That was within easy walking distance of Jerusalem, about two miles southeast of the Temple's eastern gate (John 11:18)—just over the Mount of Olives from Jerusalem's city center. Both Luke and John recorded that Jesus enjoyed hospitality in the home of this family. He went there on at least three crucial occasions in the gospels. Bethany was apparently a regular stop for Him in His travels, and this family's home seems to have become a welcome hub for Jesus during His visits to Judea.

Martha and Mary make a fascinating pair—very different in many ways, but alike in one vital respect: both of them loved Christ. By now, you're surely beginning to notice that this is the consistent hallmark of every woman whom the Bible treats as exemplary. They all point to Christ.

Everything praiseworthy about them was in one way or another centered on *Him*. He was the focus of earnest expectation for every one of the outstanding women in the Old Testament, and He was greatly beloved by all the principal women in the New Testament. Martha and Mary of Bethany are classic examples. They became cherished personal friends of Jesus during His earthly ministry. Moreover, He had a profound love for their family. The apostle John, who was a keen observer of whom and what Jesus loved, made it a point to record that "Jesus loved Martha and her sister and Lazarus" (John 11:5 NKJV).

We're not told how this particular household became so intimate with Jesus. Since no family ties are ever mentioned between Jesus' relatives and the Bethany clan, it seems likely that Martha and Mary were simply two of the many people who heard Jesus teach early in His ministry, extended Him hospitality, and built a relationship with Him that way. In whatever way this relationship began, it obviously developed into a warm and deeply personal fellowship. It is clear from Luke's description that Jesus made Himself at home in their house.

The fact that Jesus actively cultivated such friendships sheds light on the kind of man He was. It also helps explain how He managed to have an itinerant ministry in Judea without ever becoming a homeless indigent, even though He maintained no permanent dwelling of His own (Matt. 8:20). Apparently, people like Martha and Mary regularly welcomed Him into their homes and families, and He was clearly at home among His many friends.

Certainly hospitality was a special hallmark of *this* family. Martha in particular is portrayed everywhere as a meticulous hostess. Even her name is the feminine form of the Aramaic word for "Lord." It was a perfect name for her because she was clearly the one who presided over her house. Luke 10:38 speaks of the family home as *Martha's* house. That, together with the fact that her name was usually listed first whenever she was named with her siblings, implies strongly that she was the elder sister. Lazarus appears to be the youngest of the three, because he was named last in John's list of family members (John 11:5), and Lazarus rarely comes to the foreground of any narrative—including John's description of how Lazarus was raised from the dead.

Some believe Martha's position as owner of the house and dominant one in the household indicates that she must have been a widow. That's possible, of course, but all we know from Scripture is that these three siblings lived together, and there is no mention that any of them had ever been married. Nor is any hint given about how old they were. But since Mary was literally at Jesus' feet each time she appeared, it would be hard to imagine them as very old. Furthermore, the starkly contrasting temperaments of Martha and Mary seem unmellowed by much age. I'm inclined to think they were all three still very young and inexperienced. Indeed, in their interaction with Christ, He always treated them much the same way an elder brother would, and many of the principles He taught them were profoundly practical lessons for young people coming of age. A few of those lessons rise to particular prominence in the episode we will soon examine.

THREE SNAPSHOTS OF MARTHA AND MARY TOGETHER

Scripture gives three significant accounts of Jesus' interaction with this family. First, Luke 10:38–42 describes a minor conflict between Martha and Mary over how best to show their devotion to Christ. That is where we initially meet Martha and Mary in the New Testament. The way Luke described their clashing temperaments was perfectly consistent with everything we see in two later incidents recorded by John. (We'll return to focus mostly on the end of Luke 10 in this chapter because that's where the contrasting personalities of these two are seen most clearly.)

A second close-up glimpse at the lives of these two women comes in

John 11. Virtually the entire chapter is devoted to a description of how their brother Lazarus died and was brought back to life by Christ. Jesus' personal dealings with Martha and Mary in this scene highlighted their individual characteristics. Although we don't have space enough to consider the event thoroughly, we'll later return briefly just to take note of how the death and subsequent raising of Lazarus affected both Martha and Mary profoundly, but differently, according to their contrasting personalities. John gave very detailed and poignant descriptions of how deeply the sisters were distressed over their loss, how Jesus ministered to them in their grief, how He mourned with them in a profound and personal way, and how He gloriously raised Lazarus from the dead at the very climax of the funeral. More than any other act of Jesus, that one dramatic and very public miracle was what finally sealed the Jewish leaders' determination to put Him to death because they knew that if He could raise the dead, people would follow Him, and the leaders would lose their power base (John 11:45–57). They obstinately refused to consider that His power to give life was proof that He was exactly who He claimed to be: God the Son.

Martha and Mary seemed to understand that Jesus had put Himself in jeopardy in order to give them back the life of their brother. In fact, the full depth of Mary's gratitude and understanding was revealed in a third and final account where both of these women appeared together one more time. John 12 (with parallel accounts in Matthew 26:6–13 and Mark 14:3–9) records how Mary anointed the feet of Jesus with costly ointment and wiped His feet with her hair. Although both Matthew and Mark described the event, neither of them mentioned Mary's name in this context. It was nonetheless clear that they were describing the same incident we read about in John 12. Both Matthew 26:12 and John 12:7 indicated that Mary, in some sense, understood that she was anointing Jesus for burial. She must have strongly suspected that her brother's resurrection would drive Jesus' enemies to a white-hot hatred, and they would be determined to put Him to death (John 11:53–54). Jesus Himself had gone to the relative safety of Ephraim right after the raising of Lazarus, but Passover brought Him back to Jerusalem (vv. 55–56). Mary (and probably Martha as well) seemed to grasp more clearly than anyone how imminent the threat to Jesus was. That surely intensified their sense of debt and gratitude toward Him, as reflected in Mary's act of worship.

MARY, THE TRUE WORSHIPER

According to Matthew and Mark, Mary's anointing of Jesus' feet took place at the home of "Simon the leper." Of course, a person with an active case of leprosy would not have been able to *attend* a gathering like this, much less *host* it in his own home. Lepers were considered ceremonially unclean, therefore banished from populated areas (Lev. 13:45–46), so Simon's nickname must signify that he was a *former* leper. Since Scripture says Jesus healed all who came to Him (Luke 6:19), Simon was probably someone whom Jesus had healed from leprosy. (Just such an incident is described in Luke 5:12–15).

Simon also must have been a well-to-do man. With all the disciples present, this was a sizable dinner party. He may also have been an unmarried man, because Martha seems to have been acting as hostess at this gathering. Some have suggested that she might have made her living as a professional caterer. More likely, Simon was a close friend of the family, and she volunteered to serve. Lazarus was present too (John 12:2). It appears that the gathering was a close group of Jesus' friends and disciples. Perhaps it was a formal celebration of Lazarus's return from the dead. If so, this group of friends had come together mainly to express their gratitude to Jesus for what He had done.

Mary knew exactly how best to show gratitude. Her action of anointing Jesus was strikingly similar to another account from earlier in Jesus' ministry (Luke 7:36–50). At a different gathering, in the home of a different man, a Pharisee (who was coincidentally also named Simon), a woman "who was a sinner" (v. 37 NKJV)—apparently a repentant prostitute (v. 39)—had once anointed Jesus' feet and wiped them with her hair, exactly like Mary in the John 12 account. In all likelihood, the earlier incident was well known to Martha and Mary. They knew the lesson Jesus taught on that occasion: "Her sins, which are many, are forgiven, for she loved much" (v. 47 NKJV). Mary's reenactment would therefore have been a deliberate echo of the earlier incident, signifying how much she also loved Jesus and how supremely grateful to Him she was.

Both Matthew and Mark indicate that Jesus' willingness to accept such a lavish expression of worship is what finally sealed Judas's decision to betray Christ. According to John, Judas resented what he pretended to perceive as a "waste," but his resentment was really nothing more than greed. He was actually pilfering money from the disciples' treasury (John 12:4–6).

So the lives of these two women inadvertently intersected *twice* with the sinister plot to kill Jesus. The raising of their brother first ignited the plot among the Jewish leaders that finally ended with Jesus' death. Mary's munificent expression of gratitude to Jesus then finally pushed Judas over the edge.

MARTHA, THE DEVOTED SERVANT

Reluctantly setting that aside, our main focus in this chapter is that famous incident described at the end of Luke 10 when Jesus gave Martha a mild rebuke and a strong lesson about where her real priorities ought to lie. The passage is short but rich. Luke writes:

Now it happened as they went that He entered a certain village; and a certain woman named Martha welcomed Him into her house. And she had a sister called Mary, who also sat at Jesus' feet and heard His word. But Martha was distracted with much serving, and she approached Him and said, "Lord, do You not care that my sister has left me to serve alone? Therefore tell her to help me."

And Jesus answered and said to her, "Martha, Martha, you are worried and troubled about many things. But one thing is needed, and Mary has chosen that good part, which will not be taken away from her." (10:38–42 NKJV)

Martha seemed to be the elder of the two sisters. Luke's description of her behavior is one of the things that supports the idea that these three siblings were still young adults. Martha's complaint sounds callow and girlish. Jesus' reply, though containing a mild rebuke, has an almost grandfatherly tone to it.

Jesus had apparently come at Martha's invitation. She was the one who welcomed Him in, signifying that she was the actual master of ceremonies in this house. On this occasion, at least, she wasn't merely filling in as a surrogate hostess for a friend; she was plainly the one in charge of the household.

In Luke 7:36–50, when Jesus visited the home of Simon the Pharisee (where the *first* anointing of His feet took place), He was clearly under the scrutiny of His critics. The hospitality was notoriously poor on that occasion; Simon did not offer Jesus water to wash His feet or even give Him a proper greeting (Luke 7:44–46)—two *major* social snubs in that culture. The washing of a guest's feet was the first-century Middle Eastern equivalent of offering to take a guest's coat (John 13:1–7). Not to do it was tantamount to implying that you wished the guest would leave quickly. And to omit the formal greeting was tantamount to declaring him an enemy (2 John 10–11).

Martha, to her great credit, was at the opposite end of the hospitality spectrum from Simon the Pharisee. She fussed over her hostessing duties. She wanted everything to be just right. She was a conscientious and considerate hostess, and these were admirable traits. Much in her behavior was commendable.

I love the way Jesus came across in this scene. He was the perfect houseguest. He instantly made Himself at home. He enjoyed the fellowship and conversation, and as always, *His* contribution to the discussion was instructive and enlightening. No doubt His disciples were asking Him questions, and He was giving answers that were thought-provoking, authoritative, and utterly edifying. Mary's instinct was to sit at His feet and listen. Martha, ever the fastidious one, went right to work with her preparations.

THE CONFLICT BETWEEN THEM

Soon, however, Martha grew irritable with Mary. It's easy to imagine how her exasperation might have elevated. At first, she probably tried to hint in a "subtle" way that she needed help, by making extra noise—maybe moving some pots and pans around with a little more vigor than the situation really required, and then by letting some utensils or cookware clatter together loudly in a washbasin. Martha might have cleared her throat or exhaled a few times loudly enough to be heard in the next room. Anything to remind Mary that her sister was expecting a little help. When all of that failed, she probably tried to peek around the corner or walk briskly through to the dining room, hoping to catch Mary's eye. In the end, however, she just gave up all pretense of subtlety or civility and aired her grievance against Mary right in front of Jesus. In fact, she complained *to* Him and asked Him to intervene and set Mary straight.

Jesus' reply must have utterly startled Martha. It didn't seem to have occurred to her that she might be the one in the wrong, but the little scene earned her the gentlest of admonitions from Jesus. Luke's account ends there, so we're probably safe to conclude that the message penetrated straight to Martha's heart and had exactly the sanctifying effect Christ's words always have on those who love Him.

Indeed, in the later incident recorded in John 12, where Mary anointed

Jesus' feet, Martha once again is seen in the role of server. But this time *Judas* was the one who complained (John 12:4–5). He apparently tried his best to drum up a general outcry against Mary's extravagance and managed to stir some expressions of indignation from some of the other disciples (Matt. 26:8). But Martha wisely seems to have held her peace this time. She no longer seemed resentful of Mary's devotion to Christ. Martha herself loved Christ no less than Mary did, I believe. He clearly loved them both with deepest affection (John 11:5).

Some important lessons emerge from Jesus' reprimand of Martha. We would all do well to heed these admonitions.

A LESSON ABOUT THE PREFERENCE OF OTHERS OVER SELF

Jesus' gentle admonition to Martha is first of all a reminder that we should honor others over ourselves. Scripture elsewhere says, "Be kindly affectionate to one another with brotherly love, in honor giving preference to one another" (Rom. 12:10 NKJV). "Be submissive to one another, and be clothed with humility, for 'God resists the proud, but gives grace to the humble'" (1 Peter 5:5 NKJV). "Let nothing be done through selfish ambition or conceit, but in lowliness of mind let each esteem others better than himself. Let each of you look out not only for his own interests, but also for the interests of others" (Phil. 2:3–4 NKJV).

Humility had been a constant theme in Jesus' teaching, and a difficult lesson for most of His disciples to learn. Even on the night of Jesus' betrayal, each of the disciples had ignored basic hospitality rather than take a servant's role and wash the others' feet (John 13:1–7).

In the Luke 10 account, Martha's external behavior at first appeared to be true servanthood. She was the one who put on the apron and went to work in the task of serving others. But her treatment of Mary soon revealed a serious defect in her servant's heart. She allowed herself to become censorious and sharp-tongued. Such words in front of other guests were certain to humiliate Mary. Martha either gave no thought to the hurtful effect of her words on her sister, or she simply didn't care.

Furthermore, Martha was wrong in her judgment of Mary. She assumed Mary was being lazy. "Who are you to judge another's servant? To his own master he stands or falls" (Rom. 14:4 NKJV). Did Martha imagine that she, rather than Christ, was Mary's true master?

In reality, Mary was the one whose heart was in the right place. Her motives and desires were more commendable than Martha's. Jesus knew it, even though no mere mortal could ever make that judgment by observing the external behavior of the two women. But Jesus knew it because He knew the hearts of both women.

Martha's behavior shows how subtly and sinfully human pride can corrupt even the best of our actions. What Martha was doing was by no means a bad thing. She was waiting on Christ and her other guests. In a very practical and functional sense, she was acting as servant to all, just as Christ had so often commanded. She no doubt began with the best of motives and the noblest of intentions.

But the moment she stopped listening to Christ and made something other than Him the focus of her heart and attention, her perspective became very self-centered. At that point, even her service to Christ became tainted with self-absorption and spoiled by a very uncharitable failure to assume the best of her sister. Martha was showing an attitude of sinful pride that made her susceptible to several other kinds of evil as well: anger, resentment, jealousy, distrust, a critical spirit, judgmentalism, and unkindness. All of that flared up in Martha in a matter of minutes.

Worst of all, Martha's words impugned the Lord Himself: "Lord, do You not care . . . ?" (Luke 10:40 NKJV). Did she really imagine that *He* did not care? She certainly knew better. Jesus' love for all three members of this family was obvious to all (John 11:5).

But Martha's thoughts and feelings had become too self-focused.

Because of that, she also fell into an all-too-common religious trap described by Paul in his letter to the Corinthians: "They, measuring themselves by themselves, and comparing themselves among themselves, are not wise" (2 Cor. 10:12 NKJV). She turned her attention from Christ and began watching Mary with a critical eye. Naturally, it began to ruin the whole evening for Martha.

Mary, by contrast, was so consumed with thoughts of Christ that she became completely oblivious to everything else. She sat at His feet and listened to Him intently, absorbing His every word and nuance. She was by no means being lazy. She simply understood the *true* importance of this occasion. The Son of God Himself was a guest in her home. Listening to Him and worshiping Him were at that moment the very best use of Mary's energies and the one right place for her to focus her attention.

One thing that stood out about Mary of Bethany was her keen ability to observe and understand the heart of Christ. Mary's temperament seemed naturally more contemplative than Martha's. In Luke 10, she wanted to listen intently to Jesus, while Martha bustled around making preparations to serve the meal. In John 11, when Jesus arrived after Lazarus had already died, Martha ran out of the house to meet Him, but Mary remained in the house, immersed in grief (John 11:20). She was absorbed, as usual, in deep thoughts. People like Mary are not given to sudden impulse or shallow activity. Yet while Jesus had to *coax* a confession of faith from Martha (vv. 23–27)—and even that was pretty shaky (v. 39)—Mary simply fell at His feet in worship (v. 32).

Mary seemed to be able to discern Jesus' true meaning even better than any of the twelve disciples. Her gesture of anointing Him in preparation for His burial at the beginning of that final week in Jerusalem shows a remarkably mature understanding. That was the fruit of her willingness to sit still, listen, and ponder. It was the very thing that always made Mary such a sharp contrast to Martha, whose first inclination was usually to act—or react. (Martha had a lot in common with Peter in that regard.)

If Martha had truly preferred Mary over herself, she might have seen in Mary a depth of understanding and love for Christ that surpassed even her own. She could have learned much from her more quiet, thoughtful sister. *But not right now.* Martha had a table to set, a meal to get out of the oven, and "many things" she was "worried and troubled about" (Luke 10:41 NKJV). Before she knew it, her resentment against Mary had built up, and she could no longer restrain herself. Her public criticism of Mary was an ugly expression of pride.

A LESSON ABOUT THE PRIORITY OF WORSHIP OVER SERVICE

It's interesting to read this narrative and try to imagine how the average woman might respond if placed in a situation like Martha's. My strong suspicion is that *many* women would be inclined to sympathize with Martha, not Mary. After all, it would normally be considered rude to let your sister do all the hard work in the kitchen while you sit chatting with guests.

So in a real sense, Martha's feelings were natural and somewhat understandable. That may be one reason Jesus' rebuke was so mild. In normal circumstances, any older sister would think it obligatory for the younger sister to help in serving a meal to guests. In other words, what Martha expected Mary to do was, in itself, perfectly fine and good.

Nevertheless, what Mary was doing was better still. She had "chosen that good part" (Luke10:42 NKJV). She had discovered the one thing needful: true worship and devotion of one's heart and full attention to Christ. That was a higher priority even than service, and the good part she had chosen would not be taken away from her, even for the sake of something as gracious and beneficial as helping Martha prepare Jesus a meal. Mary's humble, obedient heart was a far greater gift to Christ than Martha's well-set table.

This establishes worship as the highest of all priorities for every Christian. Nothing, including even service rendered to Christ, is more important than listening to Him and honoring Him with our hearts. Remember what Jesus told the Samaritan woman at the well: God is seeking true worshipers (John 4:23). Christ had found one in Mary. He would not affirm Martha's reprimand of her, because it was Mary, not Martha, who properly understood that worship is a higher duty to Christ than service rendered on His behalf.

It is a danger, even for people who love Christ, that we not become so concerned with *doing things for Him* that we begin to neglect *hearing Him* and *remembering what He has done for us*. We must never allow our service for Christ to crowd out our worship of Him. The moment our works become more important to us than our worship, we have turned the true spiritual priorities on their heads.

In fact, that tendency is the very thing that is so poisonous about all forms of pietism and theological liberalism. Whenever you elevate good deeds over sound doctrine and true worship, you ruin the works too. Doing good works for the works' sake has a tendency to exalt self and depreciate the work of Christ. Good deeds, human charity, and acts of kindness are crucial expressions of real faith, but they must flow from a true reliance on *God's* redemption and *His* righteousness. After all, our own good works can never be a means of earning God's favor; that's why in Scripture the focus of faith is always on what God has done for us, and never on what we do for Him (Rom. 10:2–4). Observe any form of religion where good works are ranked as more important than authentic faith or sound doctrine, and you'll discover a system that denigrates Christ while unduly magnifying self.

Not that Martha was guilty of gross self-righteousness. We shouldn't be any more harsh in our assessment of her than Christ was. She loved the Lord. Her faith was real, but by neglecting the needful thing and busying herself with mere activity, she became spiritually unbalanced. Her

167

behavior reminds us that a damaging spirit of self-righteousness can slip in and contaminate even the hearts of those who have sincerely embraced Christ as their true righteousness. Martha's harshness toward Mary exposed precisely that kind of imbalance in her own heart.

Jesus' gentle words of correction to Martha (as well as His commendation of Mary) set the priorities once more in their proper order. Worship (which is epitomized here by listening intently to Jesus' teachings) is the one thing most needed. Service to Christ must always be subordinate to that.

A LESSON ABOUT THE PRIMACY OF FAITH OVER WORKS

A third vital spiritual principle goes hand in hand with the priority of worship over service and is so closely related to it that the two actually overlap. This third principle is the truth (taught from the beginning to the end of Scripture) that what we *believe* is ultimately more crucial than what we *do*.

Martha's "much serving" was a distraction (Luke 10:40 NKJV) from the "one thing" (v. 42 NKJV) that was really needed—listening to and learning from Jesus. Religious works often have a sinister tendency to eclipse faith itself. Proper good works always flow from faith and are the fruit of it. What we do is vital, because that is the evidence that our faith is living and real (James 2:14–26). But faith must come first and is the only viable foundation for true and lasting good works. All of that is wrapped up in the truth that works are not the instrument of justification; faith is (Rom. 4:4-5).

Martha seems to have forgotten these things momentarily. She was acting as if Christ needed her work for Him more than she needed His work on her behalf. Rather than humbly fixing her faith on the vital importance of Christ's work for sinners, she was thinking too much in terms of what she could do for Him.

Again, this seems to be the natural drift of the human heart. We wrongly imagine that what we do for Christ is more important than what He has done for us. Every major spiritual decline in the history of Christianity has come when the church has lost sight of the primacy of faith and begun to stress works instead. Virtually every serious doctrinal deviation throughout church history has had this same tendency at its core—beginning with the error of the Judaizers, who insisted that an Old Covenant ritual (circumcision) was essential for justification. They denied that faith alone could be instrumental in justification, and that undermined the very foundation of the gospel.

Human instinct seems to tell us that what we *do* is more important than what we *believe.* But that is a false instinct, the product of our fallen self-righteousness. It is a totally wrong way of thinking—*sinfully* wrong. We must never think more highly of our works for Christ than we do of His works on our behalf.

Of course, such a thought would never consciously enter Martha's mind. She loved Christ. She genuinely trusted Him, although her faith had moments of weakness. Still, on this occasion, she allowed her anxiety about what she must do for Christ to overwhelm her gratitude over what He would do for her.

I'm very grateful that Christ's rebuke of Martha was a gentle one. I must confess that it is very easy for me to identify with her. I love the privilege of serving the Lord, and He has blessed me with more than enough to stay busy. It is tempting at times to become swept up in the activity of ministry and forget that faith and worship must always have priority over work. In these hectic times, we all need to cultivate more of Mary's worshipful, listening spirit and less of Martha's scrambling commotion.

Martha and Mary also remind us that God uses all kinds of people. He has gifted us differently for a reason, and we're not to despise one another or look at others with contempt, just because we have differing temperaments or contrasting personalities.

Martha was a noble and godly woman with a servant's heart and a rare capacity for work. Mary was nobler still, with an unusual predisposition for worship and wisdom. Both were remarkable in their own ways. If we weigh their gifts and their instincts *together*, they give us a wonderful example to follow. May we diligently cultivate the best instincts of both of these extraordinary women.

10

MARY MAGDALENE: DELIVERED FROM DARKNESS

✣

Now when He rose early on the first day of the week, He appeared first to Mary Magdalene, out of whom He had cast seven demons.

Mark 16:9 NKJV

Mary Magdalene is one of the best-known and least-understood names in Scripture. Scripture deliberately draws a curtain of silence over much of her life and personal background, but she still emerges as one of the prominent women of the New Testament. She is mentioned by name in all four gospels, mostly in connection with the events of Jesus' crucifixion. She has the eternal distinction of being the first person to whom Christ revealed Himself after the resurrection.

Church traditions dating back to the early fathers have identified Mary Magdalene with the anonymous woman (identified only as "a sinner") in Luke 7:37–38, who anointed Jesus' feet and wiped them with her hair. But there is absolutely no reason to make that connection. Indeed, if we take the text of Scripture at face value, we have every reason to think otherwise. Since Luke first introduced Mary Magdalene by name in a completely different context (8:1–3) only three verses after he ended his narrative about the anointing of Jesus' feet, it seems highly unlikely that Mary Magdalene could be the same woman whom Luke described but did not name in the preceding account. Luke was too careful a historian to neglect a vital detail like that.

Some early commentators speculated that Mary Magdalene was the woman described in John 8:1–12, caught in the very act of adultery and saved from stoning by Christ, who forgave her and redeemed her. There is no basis for that association, either.

Mary Magdalene has also been the subject of a lot of extrabiblical mythology since medieval times. During the early Middle Ages, some of the gnostic heresies virtually co-opted the character of Mary Magdalene and attached her name to a plethora of fanciful legends. Apocryphal books were written about her, including one purporting to be Mary Magdalene's account of the life of Christ, *The Gospel of Mary.* Another, the gnostic *Gospel of Philip,* portrayed her as an adversary to Peter.

In recent years, some of those legends have been resurrected, and many of the long-discredited apocryphal stories about Mary Magdalene have been republished. She has become something of an icon for women in the "spiritual" fringe of the feminist movement who like the idea of Mary Magdalene as a kind of mythical goddess figure. Many of the ancient gnostic tales about her are well suited for that perspective. On a different front, one bestselling novel, *The Da Vinci Code* by Dan Brown, adapted several long-forgotten gnostic legends about Mary Magdalene and wove them into an elaborate conspiracy theory that included the blasphemous suggestion that Jesus and Mary Magdalene were secretly married and even had children. (According to that view, she, not the apostle John, was the beloved disciple mentioned in John 20:2 and 21:20.) Stacks of books ranging from utterly frivolous speculations to quasi-scholarly works have further revived selected gnostic fabrications about Mary Magdalene. A few highly sensationalized television documentaries have further reinforced the popularity of the revived myths.

So while Mary Magdalene is currently being talked about more than ever, much of the discussion is mere hype and hyperbole borrowed from ancient cults. What Scripture actually says about her is extraordinary enough without any false embellishment. Let's not allow this truly remarkable woman to get lost in the fog of ancient heretics' mystical and devilish fantasies.

DARKNESS

Mary Magdalene *did* have a dark past. Nothing indicates that her conduct was ever lewd or sordid in any way that would justify the common association of her name with sins of immorality. But Mary was indeed a woman whom Christ had liberated from demonic bondage. Luke introduced her as "Mary called Magdalene, out of whom had come seven demons" (Luke 8:2 NKJV). Mark 16:9 also mentioned the seven demons. It's the only detail we have been given about Mary Magdalene's past, except for a clue that we derive from her surname.

Actually, "Magdalene" is not a surname in the modern sense. She wasn't from a family that went by that name; she was from the village of Magdala. She was called "Magdalene" in order to distinguish her from the other women named *Mary* in the New Testament, including Mary of Bethany and Mary, the mother of Jesus.

The tiny fishing village of Magdala (mentioned only once by name in Scripture, in Matthew 15:39) was located on the northwest shore of the Sea of Galilee, some two or three miles north of the Roman city of Tiberias, and about five and a half miles south and west from Capernaum. (Capernaum, on the north shore of the lake, was Peter's hometown and a sort of home base for Jesus' Galilean ministry. Mary's hometown was within easy walking distance, or accessible by a short boat trip across the corner of the lake.) Jesus' ministry involved a number of exorcisms in that region. It seems to have been a hotbed of demonic activity.

173

The symptoms of demonic possession in the New Testament were varied. Demoniacs were sometimes insane, as in the case of the two demon-possessed men who lived in a graveyard and behaved so fiercely that no one dared approach them (Matt. 8:28–34; Mark 5:1–5). At least one of them, Mark tells us, was given to the nightmarish habit of deliberately mutilating himself with stones (Mark 5:5). More frequently, demonic possession was manifest in physical infirmities, such as blindness (Matt. 12:22), deafness (Mark 9:25), an inability to speak (Matt. 9:32–33), fits and seizures (Mark 1:26; Luke 9:38–40), and general infirmity (Luke 13:11–13).

Don't imagine (as many do) that the biblical descriptions of demon possession are merely crude accommodations to human superstition, as if the maladies characterized as demonic possession in the Bible were actually manifestations of epilepsy, dementia, or other purely psychological and physiological afflictions. Scripture *does* make a clear distinction between demon possession and diseases, including epilepsy and paralysis (Matt. 4:24). Demon possession involves bondage to an evil spirit—a real, personal, fallen spirit-creature—that indwells the afflicted individual. In several cases, Scripture describes how evil spirits spoke through the lips of those whom they tormented (Mark 1:23–24; Luke 4:33–35). Jesus sometimes forced the demonic personality to reveal itself in that way, perhaps to give clear proof of His power over evil spirits (Mark 5:8–14).

In every case, however, demon possession is portrayed as an affliction, not a sin, per se. Lawlessness, superstition, and idolatry undoubtedly have a major role in opening a person's heart to demonic possession, but none of the demonized individuals in the New Testament is explicitly associated with immoral behavior. They are always portrayed as tormented people, not willful malefactors. They suffered wretched indignities at the hands of evil spirits. They were all miserable, sorrowful, lonely, heartsick, forlorn, and pitiable creatures. Most of them were regarded as outcasts and pariahs by polite society. Scripture invariably presents them to us as victims with utterly ruined lives.

Such was Mary Magdalene, we can be certain. Satan tormented her with seven demons. There was nothing any mere man or woman could do for her. She was a veritable prisoner of demonic afflictions. These undoubtedly included depression, anxiety, unhappiness, loneliness, self-loathing, shame, fear, and a host of other similar miseries. In all probability, she suffered even *worse* torments, too, such as blindness, deafness, insanity, or any of the other disorders commonly associated with victims of demonic possession described in the New Testament. Whatever her condition, she would have been in perpetual agony—at least seven kinds of agony. Demoniacs in Scripture were always friendless, except in rare cases when devoted family members cared for them. They were perpetually restless because of their inability to escape the constant torments of their demonic captors. They were continually joyless because all of life had become darkness and misery for them. And they were hopeless because there was no earthly remedy for their spiritual afflictions.

That is all that can be said with certainty about the past of Mary Magdalene. Scripture deliberately and mercifully omits the macabre details of her dreadful demon-possession. But we are given enough information to know that at the very best, she must have been a gloomy, morose, tortured soul. And it is quite likely (especially with *so many* demons afflicting her) that her case was even worse. She might well have been so demented as to be regarded by most people as an unrecoverable lunatic.

DELIVERANCE

Christ had delivered her from all that. Luke and Mark seem to mention her former demonization only for the purpose of celebrating Christ's goodness and grace toward her. Without dredging up any squalid details from her past, they record the fact of her bondage to demons in a way that magnifies the gracious power of Christ.

One intriguing fact stands out about all the demonic deliverances that are recorded in Scripture: demon-possessed people never came to Christ to be delivered. Usually they were brought to Him (Matt. 8:16; 9:32; 12:22; Mark 9:20). Sometimes He called them to Himself (Luke 13:12), or He went to them (Matt. 8:28–29). On occasions when demons were already present upon His arrival, they would sometimes speak out with surprise and dismay (Mark 1:23–24; Luke 8:28).

Evil spirits never voluntarily entered the presence of Christ. Nor did they ever knowingly allow one whom they possessed to come close to Him. They often cried against Him (Luke 4:34). They sometimes caused violent convulsions in a last-gasp effort to keep the wretched souls they possessed away from Him (Mark 9:20), but Christ sovereignly drew and delivered multitudes who were possessed by demons (Mark 1:34, 39). Their emancipation from demonic bondage was always instantaneous and complete.

Mary Magdalene was one of them. How and when she was delivered is never spelled out for us, but Christ set her free, and she was free indeed. Having been set free from demons and from sin, she became a slave of righteousness (Rom. 6:18). Her life was not merely reformed; it was utterly transformed.

At one point in His ministry, Jesus gave a rather poignant illustration of the inadequacy of the religion of self-reform:

> When an unclean spirit goes out of a man, he goes through dry places, seeking rest; and finding none, he says, "I will return to my house from which I came." And when he comes, he finds it swept and put in order. Then he goes and takes with him seven other spirits more wicked than himself, and they enter and dwell there; and the last state of that man is worse than the first. (Luke 11:24–26 NKJV)

It's intriguing that Mary Magdalene herself was possessed by seven demons. Perhaps she had tried to reform her own life and learned the hard way how utterly futile it is to try to free oneself from Satan's grip. Good works and religion don't atone for sin (Isa. 64:6), and no sinner has it within his power to change his own heart (Jer. 13:23). We can make cosmetic changes (sweeping the house and putting it in order), but that doesn't remove us from the dominion of darkness into the kingdom of light. Only God can do that (1 Peter 2:9). Only the same "God who commanded light to shine out of darkness" has the power to shine "in our hearts to give the light of the knowledge of the glory of God in the face of Jesus Christ" (2 Cor. 4:6 NKJV). That is precisely what the Lord did for Mary Magdalene.

Mary owed everything to Christ. She knew it too. Her subsequent love for Him reflected the profound depth of her gratitude.

DISCIPLESHIP

Mary Magdalene joined the close circle of disciples who traveled with Jesus on His long journeys. Her deliverance from demons may have occurred relatively late in Christ's Galilean ministry. Luke is the only one of the gospel writers who names her in any connection prior to the crucifixion. Notice the context in which she is named:

> Now it came to pass, afterward, that He went through every city and village, preaching and bringing the glad tidings of the kingdom of God. And the twelve were with Him, and certain women who had been healed of evil spirits and infirmities; Mary called Magdalene, out of whom had come seven demons, and Joanna the wife of Chuza, Herod's steward, and Susanna, and many others who provided for Him from their substance. (Luke 8:1–3 NKJV)

There was certainly nothing inappropriate about Jesus' practice of allowing women disciples to be His followers. We can be certain that whatever traveling arrangements were made for the group, Jesus' name and honor (as well as the reputations of *all* the men and women in the group) were carefully guarded from anything that might hint at any reproach. After all, Jesus' enemies were looking desperately for reasons to accuse Him. If there had been any way whatsoever for them to drum up doubts about the propriety of Jesus' relationships with women, that issue would have been raised. But even though His enemies regularly lied about Him and even accused Him of being a glutton and a winebibber (Matt. 11:19), no accusations against Him were ever made on the basis of how He treated the women in His band of disciples. These were godly women who devoted their whole lives to spiritual things. They evidently had no family responsibilities that required them to stay home. If they had been in breach of any such duties, you can be certain that Jesus would not have permitted them to accompany Him. There is never the slightest hint of unseemliness or indiscretion in the way any of them related to Him.

It is true that most rabbis in that culture did not normally allow women to be their disciples. But Christ encouraged men and women alike to take His yoke and learn from Him. This is yet another evidence of how women are honored in Scripture.

Luke said Mary Magdalene and the other women were among many who "provided for Him from their substance" (Luke 8:3 NKJV). Perhaps Mary had inherited financial resources that she used for the support of Jesus and His disciples. The fact that she was able to travel with Jesus in the inner circle of His disciples may be a clue that she was unmarried and otherwise free from any obligation to parents or close family. She might well have been a widow. There is no evidence that she was a very young woman. The fact that her name appears at the head of the list of this band of women seems to indicate that she had a special place of respect among them.

Mary Magdalene remained Jesus' faithful disciple even when others forsook Him. In fact, she first appeared in Luke's gospel at a time when opposition to Jesus had grown to the point that He began to teach in parables (Matt. 11:10–11). When others became offended with His sayings, she stayed by His side. When others walked no longer with Him, she remained faithful. She followed Him all the way from Galilee to Jerusalem for that final Passover celebration. She ended up loyally following Him to the cross, and even beyond.

DISASTER

Matthew, Mark, and John all record that Mary Magdalene was present at the crucifixion. Combining all three accounts, it is clear that she stood with Mary, the mother of Jesus, Salome (mother of the apostles James and John), and another, lesser-known Mary (mother of James the Less and Joses).

There's an interesting progression in the gospel accounts. John, describing the state of affairs near the beginning of the crucifixion, said the women "stood by the cross" (John 19:25 NKJV). They were close enough to hear Him speak to John and Mary when He committed His mother to the beloved disciple's care (vv. 26–27).

But Matthew and Mark, describing the end of the ordeal, said the women were "looking on from afar" (Matt. 27:55; Mark 15:40 NKJV). As the crucifixion wore on, crowds of taunting miscreants moved in, elbowing the women back. The women probably drew back instinctively, too, as the scene became steadily more and more gruesome. It was as if they could not bear to watch—but they could not bear to leave.

They remained until the bitter end. There was nothing for them to do but watch and pray and grieve. It must have seemed the greatest possible disaster, to have the One whom they loved and trusted above all torn from their midst so violently. There they stood, in a crowd of bloodthirsty fanatics who were screaming for the death of their beloved Lord. With the screaming-mad furor of hatred at the very pinnacle of intensity, they could easily have become victims of the mob. But they never shrank away completely. They never left the scene until the bitter end. And even then, they stayed close to Jesus' body. Such was the magnetism of their loyalty and love for Christ.

In fact, it was only thanks to Mary Magdalene that the disciples even learned where Jesus' body was laid after His death. Mark records that Joseph of Arimathea asked Pilate for the body of Christ in order to give it a proper burial. Joseph had access to Pilate because he was a prominent member of the Sanhedrin, the ruling council of Jewish leaders (Mark 15:43). They were the same group who had conspired to bring Jesus to trial, condemned Him, and voted to put Him to death that very morning. Joseph, however, was a secret disciple of Jesus (John 19:38), and "he had not consented to their decision and deed" (Luke 23:51 NKJV). All four gospels record Joseph's action of retrieving Jesus' body. Mark added that Mary Magdalene and Mary the mother of Joses secretly followed Joseph to the tomb and "observed where He was laid" (Mark 15:47 NKJV).

The apostle John described how Joseph of Arimathea, together with Nicodemus (who was "a ruler of the Jews," according to John 3:1 NKJV, and therefore probably also a member of the Sanhedrin and a secret disciple), "took the body of Jesus, and bound it in strips of linen with the spices, as the custom of the Jews is to bury" (John 19:40 NKJV). John says Nicodemus had purchased about a hundred pounds of "myrrh and aloes" (v. 39 NKJV). These were scented spices and resins used by the Jews in lieu of embalming. The two men speedily anointed Jesus' body and bound Him tightly in linen strips (v. 40). They would have needed to hurry to finish the task before the Sabbath started (v. 42).

Mary Magdalene's love for Christ was as strong as anyone's. She took note of where and how He had been laid in the tomb. After all He had done for her, it must have broken her heart to see His lifeless, mangled body so poorly prepared and laid in a cold tomb. She was determined to wash and anoint His body properly. So Luke 23:55–56 says she and the other Mary began the preparation of their own burial spices before the Sabbath began. Mark 16:1 adds that they purchased still more spices as soon as the Sabbath was officially over (sundown on Saturday). First thing in the morning, they planned to give Him a burial worthy of Someone so profoundly loved.

DAYBREAK

Mary Magdalene had remained longer than any other disciple at the cross. Then she was also the first to reach His tomb at daybreak on the first day of the week. Her devotion was never more plain than in her response to His death, and that devotion was about to be rewarded in an unimaginably triumphant way.

There was evidently no thought of resurrection in Mary Magdalene's mind. She had seen up close the devastating effects of the bitter blows Jesus had received on the way to the cross. She had witnessed firsthand as His life ebbed from Him. She had watched as His lifeless body was unceremoniously wrapped in linen and hastily prepared ointment and left alone in the tomb. The one thought that filled her heart was a desire to do properly what she had seen done so hurriedly and haphazardly by Nicodemus and Joseph. (She might have recognized them as members of the hostile Sanhedrin. Otherwise, she probably did not know them at all.) She thought she was coming to the tomb for one final expression of love to her Master— to whom she knew she owed everything.

The apostle John, himself an eyewitness to some of the the dramatic events of that morning, gives the best description:

Now on the first day of the week Mary Magdalene went to the tomb early, while it was still dark, and saw that the stone had been taken away from the tomb. Then she ran and came to Simon Peter, and to the other disciple, whom Jesus loved, and said to them, "They have taken away the Lord out of the tomb, and we do not know where they have laid Him."

Peter therefore went out, and the other disciple, and were going to the tomb. So they both ran together, and the other disciple outran Peter and came to the tomb first. And he, stooping down and looking in, saw the linen cloths lying there; yet he did not go in. Then Simon Peter came, following him, and went into the tomb; and he saw the linen cloths lying there, and the handker-chief that had been around His head, not lying with the linen cloths, but folded together in a place by itself. Then the other disciple, who came to the tomb first, went in also; and he saw and believed. For as yet they did not know the Scripture, that He must rise again from the dead. Then the disciples went away again to their own homes.

But Mary stood outside by the tomb weeping, and as she wept she stooped down and looked into the tomb. And she saw two angels in white sitting, one at the head and the other at the feet, where the body of Jesus had lain. Then they said to her, "Woman, why are you weeping?"

She said to them, "Because they have taken away my Lord, and I do not know where they have laid Him." (John 20:1–13 NKJV)

Matthew 28:2 records that the rolling away of the stone was accompanied by "a great earthquake" (NKJV). We also know from Matthew and Mark that at least two other women ("the other Mary" and Salome) had come to help. They had discussed the difficulty of rolling the great stone (a massive wheel-shaped slab that rested in a trough) away from the mouth of the tomb, but by the time they arrived, the stone was already rolled away.

Mark 16:5 and Luke 24:3 both say the women went inside the sepulchre and found it empty. Mary's first inclination was to assume that someone had stolen Jesus' body. She immediately ran out of the tomb and back up the same trail she had come from, apparently planning to go for help. Before running far, though, she encountered Peter and John, on their way to the burial site. She breathlessly told them about the empty tomb, and they both took off running to see for themselves. John makes a point of recording that he outran Peter, but he stopped at the mouth of the tomb to peer inside, and Peter ran past him into the sepulchre itself. There Peter found the empty grave clothes and a headpiece folded and set aside. John joined him inside the tomb. Seeing the grave clothes still intact but empty was enough, John says, for him to believe. He and Peter left the scene immediately (Luke 24:12). It was probably at that point that the other women went into the tomb again to see for themselves (Mark 16:4).

Meanwhile, Mary Magdalene, overwrought with the new grief of thinking someone had stolen the body, remained outside the tomb alone. She stooped to peer in, and it was then that two angels appeared inside the tomb (John 20:12). Matthew, Mark, and Luke tell the story in abbreviated fashion, deliberately truncating some details. Each account gives different aspects of the story, but they are easy to harmonize. Of course, all the women saw the angels. Only one of the angels spoke. To the women inside the tomb, he said, "He is not here; for He is risen" (Matt. 28:6; see Mark 16:6; Luke 24:6 NKJV). Then the angel instructed them, "Go quickly and tell His disciples that He is risen from the dead" (Matt. 28:7 NKJV). At that point, all but Mary seem to have left. According to Matthew, "they went out quickly from the tomb with fear and great joy" (v. 8 NKJV).

Mary seemed to have remained outside the tomb, still disconsolate over the missing body. Evidently she had taken no notice of the empty grave clothes. It seems clear that she had neither heard the angel's triumphant news, nor did she understand how elated Peter and John were when they left the tomb. The angel came and spoke directly to her: "Woman, why are you weeping?" (John 20:13 NKJV).

Through her broken-hearted sobs, Mary replied, "Because they have taken away my Lord, and I do not know where they have laid Him" (John 20:13 NKJV).

It was just then that she turned and saw Jesus. At first, through her tear-filled eyes, she did not recognize Him at all. (She was not the only one who did not instantly perceive who He was after His resurrection. Later that day, according to Luke 24:13–35, two of His disciples traveled some distance with Him on the road to Emmaus before their eyes were opened to realize who He was.) His countenance was different—glorified. If He looked the way John described Him in Revelation 1:14, "His head and hair were white like wool, as white as snow, and His eyes like a flame of fire" (NKJV).

Jesus spoke: "Woman, why are you weeping? Whom are you seeking?" (John 20:15 NKJV).

Mary, thinking He was the gardener, pleaded with Him to show her where they had taken the body of Christ.

All He had to say was her name, and she instantly recognized Him. "He calls his own sheep by name . . . [and] they know his voice" (John 10:3–4 NKJV).

"Rabboni!" Mary's grief instantly turned to inexpressible joy (John 20:16 NKJV), and she must have tried to clasp Him as if she would never let Him go.

His words, "Do not cling to Me" (v. 17), testified in a unique way to the extraordinary character of Mary Magdalene. Most of us are too much like the apostle Thomas—hesitant, pessimistic. Jesus urged Thomas to touch Him, in order to verify Jesus' identity (v. 27). It is remarkable and sad—but true—that most of Jesus' disciples, especially in this postmodern age, constantly need to be coaxed nearer to Him. Mary, by contrast, did not want to let go.

Jesus thus conferred on her a unique and unparalleled honor allowing her to be the first to see and hear Him after His resurrection. Others had already heard and believed the glad news from the mouth of an angel.

Mary got to hear it first from Jesus Himself. The biblical epitaph on her life was recorded in Mark 16:9: "When He rose early on the first day of the week, He appeared first to Mary Magdalene" (NKJV).

That was her extraordinary legacy. No one can ever share that honor or take it from her. But we can, and should, seek to imitate her deep love for Christ.

11
LYDIA: A HOSPITABLE HEART OPENED

✖

Now a certain woman named Lydia heard us. She was a seller of purple from the city of Thyatira, who worshiped God. The Lord opened her heart to heed the things spoken by Paul.

Acts 16:14 NKJV

Lydia is best remembered as the original convert for the gospel in Europe. She was the first person on record ever to respond to the message of Christ during the apostle Paul's original missionary journey into Europe. Her conversion marked the earliest foothold of the church on a continent that ultimately became the hub of the gospel's witness worldwide. (Europe has only relinquished that distinction to North America in the past hundred years or so.)

Ironically, however, Lydia herself was not European. Her name was also the name of a large Asian province, which was probably the region of her birth. The capital city of Lydia was Sardis. That territory's last and best-known ruler was Croesus, who ruled in the sixth century BC and whose very name is synonymous with wealth. (He was defeated by Cyrus, ruler of Medo-Persia in Ezra's time. Cyrus used the captured wealth of Croesus to help him conquer most of the known world.) In Roman times, the once-great land of Lydia was merely one of the provinces of Asia Minor. But by the end of the apostolic age, the province of Lydia was also a thriving center of Christianity. Sardis (still the region's capital city in the apostle John's time) was home to one of the seven churches in the book of Revelation (3:1–6).

Lydia's actual hometown was the city of Thyatira. Thyatira, in the province of Lydia, was home to one of the seven churches of Revelation (2:18–29). Significantly, Thyatira was located in the very region of Asia Minor where Luke tells us Paul, Silas, and Timothy "were forbidden by the Holy Spirit to preach the word" (Acts 16:6 NKJV).

Shortly after all doors were closed to Paul for any further church-planting in Asia Minor, God sovereignly led the missionary party into Europe by means of a dream in which a Macedonian man "stood and pleaded with [Paul], saying, 'Come over to Macedonia and help us'" (v. 9 NKJV). Macedonia in those days was the name of a Roman province that covered much of the upper peninsula of Greece, extending from the Adriatic to the Aegean. The area where Paul ministered lies in modern-day Greece. (Modern Macedonia is a considerably smaller region, distinct from Greece.) "Immediately," Luke says, "we sought to go to Macedonia, concluding that the Lord had called us to preach the gospel to them" (v. 10 NKJV).

The ironies are many. Instead of reaching Lydia in the region she regarded as home, the gospel pursued her to Europe, where she was engaged in business. Although Paul saw a Macedonian man in his vision, an Asian woman became the first convert on record in Europe.

Lydia was a remarkable woman who appeared suddenly and unexpectedly in the biblical narrative, reminding us that while God's sovereign purposes usually remain hidden from our eyes, He is always at work in secret and surprising ways to call out a people for His name.

HOW THE GOSPEL CAME TO LYDIA

Lydia's story is brief but compelling. It is told in just a few verses near the start of Luke's narrative about the apostle Paul's second missionary journey. This was an extended missionary trip whose description spans Acts 15:36–18:22. Paul's main companions on that long journey were Silas and Timothy. Luke apparently joined them just before they crossed the narrow strait from Troas (in Asia Minor) into Macedonia (entering Europe). Luke's enlistment in the missionary team was signaled by an abrupt change to first-person pronouns, starting in Acts 16:10 (NKJV) ("immediately we sought to go to Macedonia"). From that point on, Luke wrote as an eyewitness. It was at that very point Lydia's story came into play.

The sovereign hand of God's providential guidance was evident to Paul's entire group. Luke didn't explain all the circumstances, but by some means they had been forbidden by the Spirit of God to journey into the heart of Asia Minor. Every other door of ministry in Asia was also closed to them (16:6–8). That's when Paul received a revelation calling him across to the European continent. God had made it perfectly clear to all that there was just one way ahead—Macedonia. They wasted no time crossing to the Greek mainland.

Luke gives a detailed account of the route they took to Macedonia: "Sailing from Troas, we ran a straight course to Samothrace [an island in the Aegean, where they harbored overnight], and the next day came to Neapolis, and from there to Philippi, which is the foremost city of that part of Macedonia, a colony. And we were staying in that city for some days" (16:11–12 NKJV). The short two- or three-day journey was mostly by sea. The route from Troas to Neapolis covered about 140 nautical miles. Neapolis was the port city adjacent to Philippi, which lay some ten miles farther inland.

Philippi took its name from Philip II of Macedon, father of Alexander the Great. It was the eastern terminus of a famous Roman road known as the Egnatian Way. Thessalonica, where Paul would later found a famous church, lay another 150 miles west, at the other end of the Egnatian Way.

In Paul's day, Philippi was a thriving, busy community at the crossroads of two trade routes (one by land via the highway from Thessalonica; the other by sea, via the port at nearby Neapolis). Luke describes Philippi as "a colony" (Acts 16:12 NKJV), which means it was a colony of Rome, with a Roman government and a large population of Roman citizens. History records that Philippi had become a Roman colony in 31 BC. That meant the city had its own local government accountable directly to Rome, completely independent of the provincial Macedonian government. Its citizens were also exempt from Macedonian taxes. So this was a prosperous and flourishing city, bustling with trade and commerce from all over the world. It was a strategic place for introducing the gospel to Europe.

Paul and company spent "some days" in Philippi, apparently waiting for the Sabbath. Paul's normal evangelistic strategy was to take the gospel first to the local synagogue, because if he went to the Gentiles first, the Jews would never listen to anything he had to say. Philippi, however, was a thoroughly Gentile town with no synagogue.

There were a few Jews in Philippi, but very few—not even enough to support a synagogue. In order to start a synagogue in any community, Jewish custom required a quorum (known as a minyan) of at least ten Jewish men (any adult males beyond the age of Bar Mitzvah would qualify). The number was supposedly derived from the biblical account of the destruction of Sodom and Gomorrah, in which God told Abraham He would spare those cities for the sake of ten righteous men (Gen. 18:32–33). But the minyan rule was a classic example of rabbinical invention. Biblical law made no such restriction.

According to the tradition, in communities without synagogues, Jewish women could pray together in groups if they liked, but men had to form a legitimate minyan before they could partake in any kind of formal, public, communal worship—including prayer, the reading of the Torah, or the giving of public blessings.

Since Philippi's Jewish community was apparently not large enough to form a legitimate minyan, Paul and his group learned the place where Jewish women gathered to pray on the Sabbath, and they went there instead. Luke writes, "On the Sabbath day we went out of the city to the riverside, where prayer was customarily made; and we sat down and spoke to the women who met there" (Acts 16:13 NKJV). The river was a small stream known as the Gangitis, just west of the town. Apparently, the small group of women who gathered there constituted the only public gathering of Jews anywhere in Philippi on a typical Sabbath day. In keeping with his principle of bringing the gospel "[to] the Jew first" (Rom. 1:16 NKJV), Paul went to the riverside to preach.

Ironically, the one woman who responded most eagerly was not Jewish at all. Lydia was a worshiper of YHWH, at least externally. But she was a Gentile, an active seeker of the true God who had not even yet become a formal Jewish proselyte. Luke described his first meeting with Lydia this way: "A certain woman named Lydia heard us. She was a seller of purple from the city of Thyatira, who worshiped God" (Acts 16:14 NKJV).

She was, in effect, a businesswoman. She sold purple dye and fancy purple cloth, manufactured by a famous guild in her hometown of Thyatira. (Archaeologists have uncovered several Roman inscriptions dating from the first century and referring to the guild of dyers in Thyatira.) The rare and expensive dye (actually more crimson than purple) was made from a spiny-shelled mollusk known as the murex. The process had been invented in ancient Tyre, and the dye was (and is still) known as Tyrian dye. Manufacturers in Thyatira had perfected a better method of obtaining the dye from the mollusks. They also had developed a less expensive dye of similar color from the root of the madder plant. This was a popular alternative to the more costly color, especially among working-class people. But the more expensive Tyrian dye was the basis for royal purple, and that substance was one of the most precious of all commodities in the ancient world. So Lydia must have been a woman of some means. The mention of a household in Acts 16:15 would indicate that she maintained a home in Philippi, most likely, with household servants. All of this confirms that she was a wealthy woman.

HOW THE GOSPEL CAPTURED LYDIA'S HEART

The manner of Lydia's conversion is a fine illustration of how God always redeems lost souls. From our human perspective, we may think we are seeking Him, that trusting Christ is merely a "decision" that lies within the power of our own will to choose, or that we are sovereign over our own hearts and affections. In reality, wherever you see a soul like Lydia's truly seeking God, you can be certain God is drawing her. Whenever someone trusts Christ, it is God who opens the heart to believe. If God Himself did not draw us to Christ, we would never come at all. Jesus was quite clear about this: "No one can come to Me unless the Father who sent Me draws him" (John 6:44 NKJV). "No one can come to Me unless it has been granted to him by My Father" (v. 65 NKJV).

The fallen human heart is in absolute bondage to sin. Every sinner is just as helpless as Mary Magdalene was under the possession of those seven demons. Romans 8:7–8 says, "The carnal mind is enmity against God; for it is not subject to the law of God, nor indeed can be. So then, those who are in the flesh cannot please God" (NKJV). We are powerless to change our own hearts or turn from evil in order to do good: "Can the Ethiopian change his skin or the leopard its spots? Then may you also do good who are accustomed to do evil?" (Jer. 13:23 NKJV). The love of evil is part of our fallen nature, and it is the very thing that makes it impossible for us to choose good over evil. Our wills are bent in accordance with what we love. We are in bondage to our own corruption. Scripture portrays the condition of every fallen sinner as a state of hopeless enslavement to sin.

Actually, it's even worse than that. It is a kind of death—an utter spiritual barrenness that leaves us totally at the mercy of the sinful lusts of our own flesh (Eph. 2:1–3). We are helpless to change our own hearts for the better.

Acts 16:14 describes Lydia as a woman "who worshiped God" (NKJV). Intellectually, at least, she already knew that YHWH was the one true God. She apparently met regularly with the Jewish women who gathered to pray on the Sabbath, but she had not yet become a convert to Judaism.

Luke recorded that Lydia "heard us" (Acts 16:14 NKJV). He used a Greek word that meant she was listening intently. She did not merely absorb the sound, but she was carefully attentive to the meaning of the words. She was not like Paul's companions on the road to Damascus, who heard the noise of a voice (Acts 9:7) but didn't understand the meaning of it (22:9). She listened with rapt attention and understanding as Paul and his companions explained the gospel message.

Her heart was truly open. She was a genuine seeker of God. But notice Luke's whole point: it was not that Lydia opened her own heart and ears to the truth. Yes, she was seeking, but even that was because God was drawing her. She was listening, but it was God who gave her ears to hear. She had an open heart, but it was God who opened her heart. Luke expressly affirms the sovereignty of God in Lydia's salvation: "The Lord opened her heart to heed the things spoken by Paul" (16:14 NKJV).

A lot of people struggle to come to grips with this truth. It is a difficult idea, but I am very glad for the truth of it. If it were not for God's sovereign work drawing and opening the hearts of sinners to believe, no one would ever be saved. This is the very thing Paul has in mind in Ephesians 2, after stressing the utter spiritual deadness of sinners, when he says salvation—all of it—is a gift of God (Eph. 2:8–9).

Did you realize that even faith is God's gift to the believer? We don't reach down into our own hearts and summon faith from within by sheer willpower. God is the one who opens our hearts to believe. Repentance is something He graciously bestows (Acts 11:18; 2 Tim. 2:25).

I think all Christians have some intuitive understanding of this truth.

That is why we pray for the salvation of our loved ones. (If salvation were solely dependent on own free-will choice, what would be the point of praying to God about it?) We also know in our hearts that we cannot boast of being wiser or more learned than our neighbors who still do not believe. We know in our hearts that our salvation is wholly and completely the work of God's grace, and not in any sense our own doing. All believers, like Lydia, must confess that it was God who first opened our hearts to believe.

The language is significant. A lot of people imagine that the doctrine of God's sovereignty has Him somehow forcing people against their wills to believe. Theologians sometimes use the expression "irresistible grace" when they describe the way God brings sinners into the kingdom. Don't imagine for a moment that there is any kind of violent force or coercion involved when God draws people to Christ. Grace doesn't push sinners against their wills toward Christ; it draws them willingly to Him—by first opening their hearts. It enables them to see their sin for what it is and empowers them to despise what they formerly loved. It also equips them to see Christ for who He truly is. Someone whose heart has been opened like that will inevitably find Christ Himself irresistible. That is precisely the meaning of the expression "irresistible grace." That is how God draws sinners to Himself. Luke's description of Lydia's conversion captures it beautifully. The Lord simply opened her heart to believe— and she did.

God's sovereign hand is seen clearly in every aspect of Luke's account. The Lord clearly orchestrated the circumstances that brought Paul to Macedonia. It was a similar providence that brought Lydia there and drew her to the riverside on a Sabbath morning with a seeking heart. It was the Spirit of God who sovereignly opened her heart, gave her spiritual ears to hear, and gave her spiritual eyes to see the irresistible appeal of Christ.

For her part, she responded instantly. God's sovereignty does not leave the sinner out of the process. Lydia heard and heeded. She willingly embraced the truth of the gospel and became a believer that very morning. She became a participant in the fulfillment of the promise made long before to Eve. The seed of the woman crushed the serpent's head for her.

HOW THE GOSPEL TRANSFORMED LYDIA'S LIFE

Lydia's faith immediately was evident in her actions. Almost incidentally, Luke said, "And when she and her household were baptized . . ." (Acts 16:15 NKJV). Remember, the meeting took place next to a river. Apparently, Lydia, like the Ethiopian eunuch, needed little encouragement to take that first step of obedience to Christ. She was baptized then and there.

Notice also that Scripture mentioned her "household." This could describe her actual family, but nothing in the context indicated she was married. It would have been highly unusual in that culture for a married woman with family responsibilities to be involved in an import-export business requiring her to travel from continent to continent. Besides, she was clearly the head of her household. It was, after all, "her" household, and verse 40 (NKJV) speaks of "the house of Lydia," signifying that she was the owner of the building.

Lydia may have been a widow. Her household most likely included servants. She may also have had grown children who lived and traveled with her. But whoever was included in the household, they all came to faith and were baptized right along with Lydia. She was already leading others to Christ. And God was graciously opening their hearts too.

Lydia was also quick to show hospitality to the missionaries. According to Luke, she "begged" them to be her guests: "If you have judged me to be faithful to the Lord, come to my house and stay" (Acts 16:15 NKJV). Luke added (with characteristic understatement), "So she persuaded us" (v. 15 NKJV).

Lydia's hospitality to these strangers who had come in the name of the Lord was commendable. Again, her eagerness to host them reminds us that she was a woman of means. We know for sure that the group included Paul, Silas, Timothy, and Luke. In all likelihood there were others. This may have been a large team. It would be no easy task, even today, to host so many strangers. Since they had no plans for where to go next (they were there, after all, to plant a church), she was offering to keep them indefinitely.

Moreover, the real cost to Lydia was potentially much higher than the monetary value of room and board for a group of missionaries. Remember that Philippi was where Paul and Silas were beaten badly, thrown in jail, and clamped in stocks. They were ultimately freed by a miraculous earthquake, and the jailer and all his household became Christians in the process. But if preaching the gospel was deemed a jailable offense, Lydia was exposing herself to possible trouble—a loss of business, bad will in the community, and even a prison sentence for herself—by housing these strangers and thus giving them a base from which to evangelize.

Her wonderful act of hospitality nevertheless opened the way for the church to penetrate Europe. Paul and the missionaries apparently stayed with Lydia for a long time. Verse 18 describes a demon-possessed woman who harassed them "for *many* days" (NKJV, emphasis added), until Paul, "greatly annoyed, turned and said to the spirit, 'I command you in the name of Jesus Christ to come out of her.' And he came out that very hour."

The possessed woman was a slave whose owners had profited greatly from her fortune-telling abilities (v. 16). After the demon left her, she could no longer do whatever trick gave her credibility as a seer. The girl's owners therefore drummed up the public opposition that soon landed Paul and Silas in jail.

After the conversion of the jailer, when Paul and Silas were finally freed, Luke said, "They went out of the prison and entered the house of Lydia; and when they had seen the brethren, they encouraged them and departed" (Acts 16:40 NKJV).

That indicates that they had been in Philippi long enough to found a fledgling church. Apparently, a number of people had responded to the gospel. Naturally, their first meeting place was Lydia's home. By opening her home to the apostle Paul, Lydia had the honor of hosting in her own living room the earliest meetings of the first church ever established in Europe! She gained that honor for herself by showing such warm hospitality to this team of missionaries whom she barely knew. She epitomized the kind of hospitality Scripture demands of all Christians.

Lydia's hospitality was as remarkable as her faith. Because of her generosity to Paul and his missionary team, the gospel obtained a solid foothold in Philippi. A few short years later, Paul penned the epistle that bears the name of that church. It is obvious from the tone of his epistle that opposition to the gospel was still strong in Philippi. But the gospel was more powerful yet, and from Philippi the testimony of Christ sounded out into all of Europe. It continues to spread to the uttermost parts of the earth, even today.

Lydia's reward in heaven will surely be great. She was a truly extraordinary woman. Like all the women in our study, everything that made her exceptional was a result of God's work in her heart. Scripture is explicit about that, especially in Lydia's case—but it is true of every woman we have studied.

EPILOGUE

The twelve women whose lives we have studied are a representative sampling of all the women whom Scripture commends. All twelve of these women—together with every other godly woman from the pages of the Bible—share several characteristics in common.

First, and most prominently, their faith and their hopes were absolutely and resolutely Christ-centered. That is the single, central, dominant truth that emerges from a study of all the godly women in Scripture, and I trust it has come through clearly as you have worked your way through this book. If these twelve women teach us anything, it is to center our lives, our faith, and our perspective of the future on Christ and Christ alone. After all, in a nutshell, that is the same response the gospel demands of us. It is not only the central theme proclaimed by the *women* of the Bible; it is the very heart of the entire biblical message.

Notice, furthermore, that the main lessons of these twelve lives are all about spiritual character and feminine virtue. The women whose lives we have been studying aren't memorable solely because of their physical beauty, their natural abilities, their personal accomplishments, or some position they attained. They aren't distinguished for any of the typical reasons celebrity is conferred on certain women these days. Most of them did not marry into any kind of fame or influence. (Did you notice that not one of our twelve extraordinary women is noteworthy exclusively because of whom she was married to? These women did not derive their identities or their reputations solely from their husbands.) Most of them did not gain any kind of celebrity at all in the eyes of the world. Among the twelve we have studied, not one of them distinguished herself through a great career, some worldly accomplishment, or anything that would even stand out in the eyes of a cultural observer. All of them were basically modest, in every sense of the word—as "is proper for women professing godliness" (1 Tim. 2:10 NKJV). Frankly, some of these women would not be deemed important at all if they were not expressly singled out in Scripture as women of faith.

So we are brought back once again to the issue of their faith. Bear this in mind: faith was the root and the quintessence of everything that made these women extraordinary. But in no case did their excellence stop with *bare* faith. The fruit of their faith was virtue. The accounts of each of them illustrate, in some significant way, a particular moral quality or spiritual trait that is worthy of emulation. With Eve, it was her perseverance in faith and expectation, even after her world had been totally shattered by her own sin. In Sarah's case, it was her steadfast hope that persevered against unbelievable obstacles. The lesson of Rahab's life is seen in the example of her remarkable conversion, because she reminds us of how dramatically God's grace can rebuild a sin-ravaged life. Ruth was a living example of devotion, love, trust, and humility. Hannah exemplified the dedication of motherhood and the importance of making one's home a place where God is honored above all. Mary, the mother of Christ, was a model of humble submission. Anna was an apt illustration of how to be a faithful witness to

200

the grace and glory of God. The Samaritan woman personified an eager response to the gospel message. Martha and Mary embodied the twin virtues of worship and service, prompted by deep devotion to Christ. Mary Magdalene was a living example of how Christ's deliverance and forgiveness prompts great love (Luke 7:47). And Lydia is best remembered for a heart that was wide open to Christ.

Not one of those women was perfect, of course. Their flaws and failures are evident, too, and those are also recorded for our admonition (1 Cor. 10:8–11). The sins of the saints in Scripture are always recounted with simple candor and never in a way that excuses or glorifies the wrongdoing. While standing as a rebuke to our sin, such stories also comfort us with the reminder that throughout history, God has used imperfect vessels, "that the excellence of the power may be of God and not of us" (2 Cor. 4:7 NKJV). After all, Christ came to seek and to save the lost—not the righteous, but sinners (Luke 19:10; Mark 2:17). These women all depict the truth of that promise, and that certainly ought to be a rich encouragement when we consider our own fallenness.

To sum up, everything that made these women extraordinary was ultimately owing to the work of the glorious Savior whom they loved and served. *God* was the truly extraordinary one, and He was simply conforming these women to their Savior's likeness (Rom. 8:29).

Extraordinary as they seem, what God was doing in their lives is really no different from what He does in the life of every true believer: "But we all, with unveiled face, beholding as in a mirror the glory of the Lord, are being transformed into the same image from glory to glory, just as by the Spirit of the Lord" (2 Cor. 3:18 NKJV).

May the extraordinary results of that process be the everyday experience of your life.

CHAPTER 1—EVE

1. What distinguishes Eve from all other women? Why did God create
   her? *She was the archetype of woman, of innocence. All other women are marred by the original sin. She was made as companion to Adam*

2. The way Eve was created speaks of Eve's fundamental equality with
   Adam. What does this mean to you? How do you understand the
   duty and role of women? *Eve was created from Adam's own body after he was put to sleep.*

3. Read Matthew 19:4–6. What did Jesus say about the relationship
   between men and women and what does that mean today?

4. In what ways was Eve a peer to Adam? In what ways were they
   different? What does this say about the marriage relationship
   today?

Symbiotic

equal importance

5. On page 7, John MacArthur says that the wife is "subordinate, yet equal" to the husband. What does this mean and how can this be a reality in your life? *roles/purposes are different, yet just because different ≠ one better than other*

6. Read Genesis 3:1–7. In what ways is your temptation similar to Eve's temptation? What process does Satan use to tempt you?

7. How can your personal Bible study help you defend yourself against temptation? *it is still my responsibility to... see p. 17✗*

8. The two most important relationships to a woman were the focus of the curse as a result of Eve's sin. What were these relationships and how important are these relationships to you? *husband, children*

9. What life principles did you learn from the study of Eve's life? How will you apply these principles to your life? *the attempt to shift blame has never changed or left the human race.*

Chapter 2—Sarah

1. What are your first thoughts about Sarai (or Sarah)? *old woman with a baby.*

2. We first discover Sarah when she was 65 years old. At that time she was beautiful but had no children. Why was it so important that a woman have children? *to further the line. To establish an heir.*

3. Review the material on pages 28–29. List Sarah's strengths and weaknesses. Now list your strengths and weaknesses. In what ways are you and Sarah similar? In what ways are you different? *She is faithful. Yet she was foolish.*

4. Because she was childless, Sarah is characterized as frustrated and

resentful. When you don't get what you expect, what words can be used to characterize the way you act? Is this a good thing or a bad thing? Explain your response. *Sulky. frustrated, disappointed.*

5. Sarah's actions reveal that she was totally devoted to her husband. Your life reveals the people and/or things to which you are totally devoted. What does your life say is important to you?

   people .

6. In spite of her years of childlessness, Sarah remained confident that God would do what He promised to do. Your life is characterized by hope. For what are you hoping? How confident are you that God will do what you expect? *for animosity towards others to be squelched.*

7. Read Genesis 17:20–21. How do you think Sarah felt when she heard these words?

8. What was significant about Sarah's laughter in Genesis 18:15? How important is it that we be honest with God? *She laughed inside, not audibly.*

9. What life principles did you learn from the study of Sarah's life? How will you apply these principles to your life?

   Being faithful. Also obedient.

CHAPTER 3—RAHAB

1. As far as we know, Rahab was a willing participant in her sinful lifestyle. If judged by society's standards, she would have been an outcast. What are some reasons we cast people aside? Are we justified in doing so? *-NO. Casting people aside gives us the false notion of "being better."*

2. What about Rahab made her one God chose to spare? *her faith.*

3. Read Joshua 2:1–7. What role did Rahab play in the Israelites' conquest of the Promised Land? Why was her involvement so important? *instrumental role - She was an unlikely candidate -*

4. Rahab lied to cover for the spies. There was nothing right about her lying. Could God have accomplished His purposes through her telling the truth about the spies? Explain your response. *Yes. of course - Shadrach, Meshach, Abednago in the furnace*

5. Lying was a way of life in Rahab's world. How important is it that we teach and learn God's principles? *It is very important. Lies are never promoted by God.*

6. Something inside Rahab made her respond to the spies favorably. What does the Holy Spirit prompt you to do that is out of character for you? *to stop and be kind. To be generous with money*

7. Read Joshua 2:8–14. What was the relationship between Rahab's fear and her faith? How would you describe this relationship in your life? *Her fear fortified her faith.*

8. What is Rahab's legacy? What does this teach us about God's ability to use us even when we've lived in ways that were displeasing to Him? *We're never too bad for God's grace.*

9. What life principles did you learn from the study of Rahab's life? How will you apply these principles to your life? *Strive for stronger faith. Reliance on faith.*

CHAPTER 4—RUTH

1. Ruth's story begins with a description of her condition. How would you describe your present condition?

206

2. Read Ruth 1:6-14. How would you describe Ruth to someone who had never heard of her?

3. Ruth expressed her commitment to Naomi and to God. In doing so, she distanced herself from the gods of her past. From what "gods" of the past do you need to be separated?

4. Naomi's faith obviously influenced Ruth. How does your faith affect other people? Do you encourage people toward God or away from Him? Explain.

5. Ruth returned to Bethlehem in order to help support Naomi. Do you have this kind of relationship with another female? Why or why not?

6. Why did Boaz feel compassion on Naomi and Ruth? Boaz is called the deliverer. Describe your first encounter with your "Deliverer."

he knew of Ruth's loyalty to Naomi

7. Boaz paid a price to redeem Ruth. How did this change Ruth's perception of her value? What is your value to God based on the price He paid to redeem you?

8. When Boaz redeemed Ruth, the contract was irrevocable. How does this compare to your relationship with God? Why is it irrevocable?

9. What life principles did you learn from the study of Ruth's life? How will you apply these principles to your life?

CHAPTER 5—HANNAH

1. Read 1 Samuel 1:24–28. How has your life been affected by the

✓spiritual devotion of your parents? How will you affect future generations?

✓2. Like Sarah, Hannah was childless. What does her willingness to give her son to God's service say about her priorities? What does your daily life say about your priorities?

3. Hannah "understood that motherhood is the highest calling God can bestow on any woman.", What is your reaction to that statement? *I believe it, but not everyone gets to experience it to achieve it*

4. Hannah was used by God to provide a leader when Israel was in desperate need of godly guidance. How is God using you? *only He knows. I sure don't.*

5. "The love between husband and wife is the real key to a thriving family.... The properly situated family has *marriage* at the center; families shouldn't revolve around the children." Why is this statement true? What adjustments do you need to make in your attitude toward marriage and children?

6. What did you learn from your parents about love, self-sacrifice, integrity, virtue, sin, sympathy, compassion, understanding, and forgiveness? What are you teaching others in these areas? *some bad ideas!!*

7. Hannah's prayer life demonstrated the depth of her love for God. What does your prayer life say about your love for God? *my prayer life is deficient.*

8. Hannah had a deep love for heaven, her husband, and her home. Because of this, God rewarded her with a fulfilling life. Is your life fulfilling? What is the connection between your fulfillment and your love for heaven, your home, and your husband? *Parts of my life are fulfilling.*

9. What life principles did you learn from the study of Hannah's life? How will you apply these principles to your life?

I need to pray more often.

CHAPTER 6—MARY

1. Mary is one of the most well-known women of the Bible and of history. What qualities do you most often associate with Mary's life?

humble, lowly, innocent, loyal, faithful, blessed, joyful

2. Read Luke 1:28–35. In this passage, God's incredible plan for Mary is revealed. What is God's incredible plan for your life and how has it been revealed to you?

no idea. To simply be a child of God.

3. In accepting her role as a pregnant virgin, Mary accepted the fact that people would think badly of her. Are you more concerned about pleasing God or people? Explain your response.

the pleasing of people is a dangerous trap often & in conflict w/ pleasing God.

4. Mary and Elizabeth were on the same page spiritually. With whom do you share a deep spiritual bond? How important is this relationship to your spiritual development?

my friends from church. It's critical.

5. Mary's natural response to God's activity in her life was a sincere attitude of worship. What is your natural response to God's work in your life? How important to you is an attitude of worship?

it's very important. Makes life better.

6. Mary yielded Jesus to God's purposes. It is vital that we yield those inside our sphere of influence to God's purposes. Who are those people you are yielding to God and what is God doing through their lives?

I yield my mother, my sister.

7. Ultimately, Mary had to watch her Son die on a Roman cross.

How do you think she felt as these events unfolded? Do you think she ever questioned God's purpose for Jesus? Why or why not?

Excruciating pain. She probably question

8. Mary never claimed to be anything more than a humble servant of God. In what ways can you become a humble servant in your daily life? Which of your priorities might God change or eliminate?

I would change my job - eliminate it.

9. What life principles did you learn from the study of Mary's life? How will you apply these principles to your life?

I am very far from true allegian to what God wants for me.

CHAPTER 7—ANNA

1. Read Luke 2:36–38. What is your initial impression of Anna?

devoted, faithful, lowly

2. Because Anna had hopes and dreams that were rooted in her understanding of Scripture, she was spiritually focused. In what are your hopes and dreams rooted? What is your primary focus? *God*

Being aligned w/ God.

3. Anna was a prophetess. What does that term mean? In what ways do you proclaim God's Word to others? *service & actions before spoken words.*

4. Luke 2:37 tells us that Anna did not depart from the temple. What does this say about the importance she placed on her relationship with God? How do you compare to her example? *Her relationship was her whole focus.*

5. Anna had been praying and fasting for a long time. How do you think she felt when she realized that Jesus was the Messiah?

joyful.

6. We don't know what happened to Anna after the experience described in Luke 2. We can only imagine that she told everyone

210

she knew about God's revelation. What do you tell everyone you
know? If their encounter with you is their only spiritual encounter,
what are they learning?

7. Anna's spiritual life would be described as focused and consistent.
How would you describe your spiritual life?

whirlwind - constantly being pulled in oth ways

8. Anna left a legacy of devotion to God. What is the legacy of your
life? What do you need to change so that your legacy will be
similar to that of Anna? *no idea.*

9. What life principles did you learn from the study of Anna's life?
How will you apply these principles to your life? *simplify.*

CHAPTER 8—THE SAMARITAN WOMAN

1. What are some reasons Jesus had to avoid the Samaritan woman?
Why did Jesus choose to engage her in conversation?

2. There were plenty of legitimate reasons for Jesus to avoid the
Samaritan woman. In what ways has Jesus gone out of His way to
affect your life?

3. Why did Jesus choose to reveal His identity as the Messiah at this
time in this place? Why did Jesus choose to reveal Himself to you?

4. The Samaritan woman was surprised that Jesus spoke to her.
Whom might be surprised by your initiating a conversation
regarding spiritual matters?

5. When Jesus told the woman to get her husband, He revealed that

His knowledge of her wasn't limited by her self-disclosure. What does this tell you about God's knowledge of the details of your life?

6. After her conversation with Jesus, the woman was dramatically transformed. In what ways has your life been changed by your relationship with Jesus?

7. The religious authorities rejected Jesus; the outcasts accepted Him. Describe your spiritual condition as either religion or a relationship. Which is easiest to maintain? Which is most beneficial to you?

8. The people of the town first believed because they saw the change in the woman. Later their faith was strengthened as they met Jesus. Is your faith based on your personal encounter with Jesus or on your encounter with people who know Him? What is the difference?

9. What life principles did you learn from the study of the Samaritan woman's life? How will you apply these principles to your life?

CHAPTER 9—MARTHA AND MARY

1. Even though they had different ways to exhibit it, Martha and Mary both loved Jesus. How do you express your love for Jesus?

2. Read Luke 10:38–42. What is the point of this story? How could the conflict between Martha and Mary have been avoided?

3. Mary is identified as the true worshiper. What elements of Mary's worship are parts of your worship? In what ways does your worship differ from that of Mary?

4. Martha is identified as a devoted servant. How does your service to God compare to the service Martha demonstrated? Are you a real servant of Jesus or a fan of Jesus? Explain your response.

5. The conflict between Martha and Mary was a reflection of the conflict between the love for others and the love for self. Consider your daily life. Are you more interested in meeting your own needs or in meeting the needs of others? In what ways can you be more focused on the needs of others?

6. Why is there a priority of worship over service? How does authentic worship affect your attitude toward service?

7. Do you prefer doing things for Jesus or spending time knowing Jesus? Would your daily schedule back up your response? Why or why not?

8. Why is faith preferred over works? What are three things you can do to develop your faith and help it grow?

9. What life principles did you learn from the study of the lives of Martha and Mary? How will you apply these principles to your life?

CHAPTER 10—MARY MAGDALENE

1. Mary Magdalene had a dark past. Jesus had liberated her from demonic bondage. From what have you or from what do you need to be liberated? How would your life change because of your liberation?

2. What is the difference between being tormented with an affliction and choosing to live in sinful rebellion? In what ways are you rebellious toward God?

3. Luke and Mark celebrated Christ's goodness and grace toward Mary Magdalene. When was the last time you celebrated Christ's goodness and grace toward you? What keeps you from celebrating it more often?

4. Mary Magdalene's love for Jesus was a direct result of her authentic faith in Him. Would you be characterized in a similar way? Why or why not?

5. It is interesting that Mary Magdalene remained faithful to Jesus even after His disciples deserted Him. Her devotion to Christ was without compromise. In what ways are you tempted to compromise your faith? What can you do to prevent that from happening?

6. Mary Magdalene was the first to reach the tomb of Jesus. How was her faith rewarded?

7. Read John 20:16. How did Mary Magdalene recognize Jesus? If Jesus spoke to you, would you recognize His voice? Why or why not?

8. Jesus appeared first to Mary Magdalene. Some might say that her faith was more intense because she had been forgiven so much. Do you love God in proportion to the forgiveness you've received? Why or why not?

9. What life principles did you learn from the study Mary Magdalene's life? How will you apply these principles to your life?

CHAPTER 11—LYDIA

1. Lydia was a businesswoman who devoted her life to God. Is your life devoted more to God or to your own pursuits? Explain your response.

2. Though Lydia was seeking God, she did not know God. Are you a seeker or a knower? Explain the point in time at which you were transformed.

3. Lydia is a classic example of the fact that good people who do not know Jesus Christ as Savior will spend eternity separated from God in a place called hell. Do you know any "good" people? What should be your attitude toward them?

4. Grace draws people to God. Explain how you were drawn to God. How might God use you to draw others to Himself?

5. When Lydia was transformed, it affected more than her. Who are those people within your circle of influence? What are you doing to influence them toward deeper relationships with God?

6. Lydia became known for her hospitality—a spiritual gift. Which spiritual gift is most evident in your life? For what purposes are you using your gift?

7. Lydia apparently became a key layperson in the church at Philippi. What is your role in your church? How might God be able to use you through your church?

8. What began in Philippi affected the entire world. What might God

be starting in your heart and life that will affect people for generations to come in places you've never seen?

9. What life principles did you learn from the study Lydia's life? How will you apply these principles to your life?

About the Author

J OHN MACARTHUR, one of today's foremost Bible teachers, is the author of numerous best-selling books that have touched millions of lives. He is pastor-teacher of Grace Community Church in Sun Valley, California, and president of The Master's College and Seminary. He is also president of Grace to You, the ministry that produces the internationally syndicated radio program Grace to You and a host of print, audio, and Internet resources—all featuring John's popular, verse-by-verse teaching. He also authored the notes in *The MacArthur Study Bible,* which has been awarded the Gold Medallion and has sold more than 500,000 copies. John and his wife, Patricia, have four children (all married), who have given them fourteen grandchildren.

For more details about John MacArthur and all his
Bible-teaching resources,
contact Grace to You at:

800-55-GRACE
or
www.gty.org

NOTES

1. Tertullian, *On the Apparel of Women,* book II, chapter 11.
2. Ibid, chapter 12.
3. Ibid, chapter 13.
4. Chrysostom, *Letter to a Young Widow,* 2.